Too Amazing for Coincidence

Strengthened in Faith

Too Amazing for Coincidence

True Stories of God's Mysterious Ways

Strengthened in Faith

EDITORS OF GUIDEPOSTS

Too Amazing for Coincidence: Strengthened in Faith

Published by Guideposts
100 Reserve Road, Suite E200
Danbury, CT 06810
Guideposts.org

Copyright © 2024 by Guideposts. All rights reserved.

This book, or parts thereof, may not be reproduced, stored in a retrieval system, or transmitted in any form or by any means, electronic, mechanical, photocopying, recording, or otherwise, without the written permission of the publisher.

Cover and interior design by Judy Ross Graphic Design
Cover photo ©YOTUYA iStock/Getty Images
Typeset by Aptara, Inc.

ISBN 978-1-961251-66-3 (hardcover)
ISBN 978-1-961442-33-7 (softcover)
ISBN 978-1-961251-67-0 (epub)

Printed and bound in the United States of America

Contents

Deliver This Message – *Doug Baker, as told to Mindy Baker*.........1
Strong Like a Bunny – *Linda S. Clare*............................5
When Grace Wore Yellow Knickers – *Linda Duty*................9
The Place I Most Wanted to See – *Marlene Kropf*.................15
The French Grocery Store Miracle – *Mary DeMuth*...............20
More Prayer, More Power! – *Joe Fletcher*........................25
A Car, a Wedding, and a Post – *Ashley Kappel*....................31
Where He Guides – *Renee Mitchell*...............................34
Beyond a Pocket-Dial – *Celeste Huttes*..........................38
Tired Tents – *David Wylie*.......................................40
A Love Note Named Brooke – *Dee Dee Parker*....................45
Full Circle – *Danielle Germain, as told to Elsa Kok Colopy*........49
Though I Walk through the Valley – *Kim Taylor Henry*...........54
Heavenly Hope in the Heat of July – *Amy Catlin Wozniak*........59
O Christmas Tree – *Ronald F. Lazenby*..........................65
All of My Ways – *Betty Meissner*.................................68
"Who Cooks for You?" – *Louis Lotz*..............................75
A Job Out of the Blue – *Raylene Nickel*..........................78
The Forgotten Skillet and the Iron – *Lynne Hartke*...............84
She Casually Stepped Out of the Crowd – *Grace Assante*..........90
A Connection across Oceans – *Lynn Spotts Carmichael*...........96
The Perfect Road Trip – *Amanda Pennock*........................99
Father's Day – *David Stauffer, as told to Kathleen Stauffer*........104
Sean's Text Message – *Jinx MacMillan*...........................107
Against the Current – *Shirley Gould*............................112
A New 20-Year Friend – *D'Ann Mateer*..........................115
The Unexpected Dog – *Lori Stanley Roeleveld*...................120
A Thread of Blue – *Rhoda Blecker*...............................125
Who in the World Is Joe Montana? – *Roberta Messner*...........129

She's Going to Be OK – *Jo Ann Fore* 134
The Day a Lunch Meeting Provided More than
  Just a Meal – *Laura R. Bailey* 140
Spring Break Reunion – *Jesse Neve* 144
Never Too Late – *Shirley E. Leonard* 147
How Crossing the Street Changed Two Lives
  and a Church – *Laura D. Garry* 151
A Cousin Connection – *Ronald F. Lazenby* 158
I'm Not Writing My Own Story – *Sarah Greek* 161
The Gift of a Life that is Different than You
  Planned – *Laura R. Bailey* 168
The Best Mistake I Ever Made – *Laura Yeager* 172
The Turn Around – *Sohani Faria* 175
Saved by a Dream – *Ingrid Skarstad* 184
Easter Moon Rising – *Jennifer Clark Vihel* 189
Picture Perfect – *Roberta Messner* 192
God Knew What I Needed – *Rebecca Hastings* 197
Until the End of the Week – *Nancy Shelton,
  as told to Marci Seither* 200
A Timely Coincidence – *Marilyn Turk* 205
A Wink from God – *Sara Etgen-Baker* 208
A Ride Home – *John Seither, as told to Marci Seither* 213
Now That I'm Sixty-Four – *Linda Marie Cumbie* 217
Little Prayer, Big Blessing – *Loraine McElhaney* 220
A Girl Named Beth – *Kristen West* 224
A Mother's Day Connection – *Glenda Ferguson* 228
God Is Always Listening – *Jesse Neve* 233
The Path that Led Me to My Perfect Pet – *Sarah Cole* 236
No Better Name for a New Friend – *Beth Gormong* 240
An Amazing Gift – *Isabella Parker* 243

Acknowledgments...247

Deliver This Message

Doug Baker, as told to Mindy Baker

For we walk by faith, not by sight.
—2 Corinthians 5:7 (CSB)

In the early morning hours of Thanksgiving Day, I suddenly awoke with an urgency to pray for a man whose first name was Bob, a prominent community leader. There was no reason I should have thought of him at that moment. Our families shared a friendship in the past, but we hadn't had any recent communication.

At first I shrugged off the impulse, rolled over, and tried to go back to sleep. I tossed and turned, but instead of fading, the urge to pray grew stronger. I finally relinquished the idea of a few more moments of rest. I would obey. I would pray.

I began praying for this man's family. I asked the Lord for safety, for health, and for the Lord's blessing on their lives. But the Lord urgently impressed on my heart that I was to pray for this man specifically. "Why?" I asked the Lord. "I haven't had a conversation with Bob in years. Why now? Is it an emergency?"

No direct answer came, so in faith I continued praying. I prayed that God would bless Bob's health, his marriage, and his job. I prayed that God would meet him at the point of any crisis he was currently going through, whether it be spiritual, emotional, or physical. I ended by praying that Bob would have a unique sense of God's presence in this moment, wherever he was. *He's probably asleep in his bed,* I thought to myself, looking at my cell phone to see what time it was.

I rolled over in the bed and closed my eyes, fully intending to go back to sleep. But prayer was not all that God wanted from me on this particular morning. He desired for me to take further action. The directions God impressed on my heart were clear: I was to get in my car and go to Bob's house. "Lord, really?" I protested. "You can't be serious."

As I got out of bed and dressed in the dark, the battle in my mind was fierce. "What will I say when I get there?" No answers or clarification came. My will protested. First, it was Thanksgiving morning. Second, this was not the type of thing that I normally did. Wouldn't he think I was crazy?

I got in my car and drove to their residence. When I turned into their neighborhood, my heart pounded and my thoughts raced. I hoped the house would be dark and that no one would be home. But when I arrived, there were multiple cars in the driveway, and I could see a light was on in the kitchen. *So much for no one being home.*

What would I say? God still hadn't revealed that important little detail. I pulled up to their house and whispered. "Lord, I am Your servant. Please help me do what You are asking me to do." I got out of my vehicle and slowly walked to their door. I took a deep breath and knocked. No one answered. I exhaled and blew out a deep breath. I knocked again. Only the brisk morning air and silence greeted me. Just as I started to give up and turn to go, the door opened and there he was. "Doug

Baker! It's been a while. Is everything OK?" He gave no indication that he was in crisis or inner turmoil or in need of prayer, but I pushed forward with the awkwardness of the moment.

"Hi Bob, er . . . um . . ." I stammered. "I don't normally do this, but God woke me up this morning and told me to pray for you." Bob didn't answer, nor did his face reveal his thoughts. But thankfully, in that moment, the Spirit revealed to me what He wanted me to say. "I'm supposed to tell you that everything is going to be OK," I blurted out. I don't honestly remember exactly what else I said, but though my words lacked eloquence, they were delivered with sincerity.

The directions God impressed on my heart were clear: I was to get in my car and go to Bob's house. "Lord, really?" I protested. "You can't be serious."

"That means a lot," he said. "Thank you."

That was it. No fireworks, no tears, no explanation. Bob and I exchanged a few more words and then I got into my car and drove home, wondering if I had made a fool out of myself. *I guess they'll have plenty to talk about around the Thanksgiving dinner table this year.* But in my heart, I felt relieved. *I obeyed You, Lord. I entrust my embarrassment into Your hands.*

When I got home, I woke up my wife and told her all that had transpired. "You did what?" she asked in disbelief.

"I obeyed God," I said. "That's what matters."

The following Monday, after a long holiday weekend, Bob's wife sought my wife out at work. With tears in her eyes, she said, "Your husband's message for Bob was a miracle. God used Doug to deliver hope to our hearts. We had both been up all night in prayer, pleading with God for an answer in a crisis we are facing. We desperately needed to hear from the Lord, and we will never forget the comfort we received that morning. When Bob came in from answering the door, he broke down in the kitchen sobbing." She went on to explain how Bob had called all of their kids down to the kitchen that morning and told them about the message. He had also repeated the experience to many family members on Thanksgiving Day.

Though I never learned what kind of crisis the family had been facing, hearing what Bob's wife said humbled me and reminded me of how important it is to obey God and listen to His voice. God is sovereign over every detail of our lives, including His ability to use us to comfort others in their desperation.

Strong Like a Bunny

Linda S. Clare

He rescued me from my powerful enemy, from my foes, who were too strong for me.
—Psalm 18:17 (NIV)

My husband, Brad, is one of the strongest men I know. An ex-Marine, he made it through battles in the Vietnam War. He's a decorated veteran, and for 45 years, he's put up with his wife—me. But one early morning, he stood outside, wondering what he had left to live for.

A year earlier, he'd survived a heart attack, only to suffer a complication that put him on kidney dialysis for life. The dialysis itself was brutal, and while he soldiered on, we nearly lost him more than once. That morning, standing there in his robe and slippers, my proud Marine was as depressed as I'd ever seen him.

Just the day before, he'd sat with his head bowed, admitting that he was so very tired. Tired of all the medical probing and poking. Tired of the relentless dialysis routine, four-hour sessions four days per week. Just tired. He looked up at me. "I don't know why I'm even still here," he said.

I tried to reassure him. "You're here for me! Remember before we married, we promised each other that we'd be holding hands in our nineties." I choked back a tear. "You can't break your promise."

He smiled, but I could tell he was still depressed. I made a mental note to report his symptoms to the doctor.

The next day, it wasn't even 7 a.m. when Brad burst into the kitchen, still in his robe. He looked out of breath. "I think the neighbor's pet bunny got loose," he said. "I'm going over to ask them to check."

Before I could ask a question, he was gone.

I quickly dressed and hurried across the street. Brad and our neighbor stood on their driveway. The neighbor held a wire cage with a light brown rabbit squirming inside. *Oh good*, I thought, *he found their bunny.*

But as I listened to the men talking, I realized I'd been wrong. The neighbor's bunny was just fine.

Brad laughed, that deep and wonderful laugh I love. "I was standing out there, when this rabbit came hopping across my yard," he said. "I thought yours was loose, so I chased it down the street with my fishing net." He blew out his breath. "She gave me a run for my money, but I caught her."

I spoke up. "But if that's not their bunny in the cage, whose is it?" She was clearly a domestic rabbit, and she was beautiful— creamy butterscotch on her back, with lop-ears that hung down. White on her underside, with the cutest white cottontail.

The guys looked at each other and then at me. Brad shrugged. "I don't know," he said. "I guess she's our bunny now."

I wasn't so sure. We put up flyers and I called every humane society and rabbit rescue in the area. No one claimed her, and the organizations said that it's common for bunnies to get dumped—they often start out as Easter gifts but are then abandoned somewhere outdoors when they are no longer fun or easy to care for. My heart broke, and I thanked God for sending us this furry rabbit friend.

When it became clear that this stray bunny wasn't going to be claimed, we bought a hutch, and Brad named her Bun Bun.

Over the next few months, Brad worked to build Bun Bun a bigger enclosure. He wanted her to be able to run around, and in the hutch she could barely turn around. He bought a greenhouse kit, fortified it with sturdy fencing, and added a gate. Brad outfitted Bun Bun's mansion with a heat lamp and

---

Brad shrugged. "I don't know," he said. "I guess she's our bunny now."

---

a cooling fan, depending on the weather. And he used artificial turf so that he could lie down with his new pet, who loved to have her long ears stroked.

Through the long summer, I noticed how much happier my Marine seemed to be. He loved to let Bun out of her enclosure during the day and watch as she hopped and grazed and binked, leaping straight up. We got good exercise and a lot of laughs trying to corral her back into her house in the evening, holding brooms while chasing her around the backyard. She loved to lead us on merry chases and then run into her house. Brad never seemed to tire of her antics, and spent a lot of time with her, eventually coaxing her up onto his chest for a nap.

By the time the leaves began to change, Bun Bun was like a family member. When she became critically ill, Brad didn't hesitate to shell out thousands for surgery. A few times a week, I walked the neighborhood, picking dandelion leaves for her dinner. None of us minded our bunny chores—we couldn't resist that wrinkly sniffing bunny nose or those deep brown eyes. When she was happy, she purred by buzzing her back teeth. And when she wanted to say "I love you," she gave us a bath with her cute little pink tongue.

Bunnies do require a lot of care to keep them healthy and happy. But the love and uplift that this one little stray provides has made all the difference for a seriously ill veteran. Instead of hanging his head and wondering what he has to live for, he knows what to do every day. Early in the morning, while he's still in his robe and slippers, he takes breakfast to his bunny friend and strokes her silky ears as she eats. He's able to thank God daily for the gift that God sent hopping into his life—a seemingly chance encounter that saved him from a very dark mental place. He's still one of the strongest people I've ever known, but he'll always be a softie for a rescue rabbit named Bun Bun.

When Grace Wore Yellow Knickers

Linda Duty

You've been a shelter in the storms of life
A shield surrounding me
And I thank You for the mercy You provide
—Clint Brown, "If Not for Grace"

The news gutted my husband, Russ, and me. On that March morning in 1977, we sat on a vinyl sofa in a tiny exam room at West Virginia University Hospital. We'd driven four hours to hear a doctor speak a word that explained our 14-month-old son's bruising and struggle to walk. The word no parent ever expects to hear. Dreads with every fiber of their being. Refuses to believe when they do hear it.

Cancer. Our only child, Chris, the answer to our dreams, had leukemia. It would be a miracle if he survived.

The what-ifs were the worst. What if the chemo and radiation didn't work? Or last? And the unspeakable question: What if God calls Chris home to be with Him?

When you have a child who's sick, you worry every single moment. As the years went by, we did plenty of that. Through every treatment, every test, every sniffle, every illness that every kid has. Sometimes the fear and doubt got the best of us. But one Sunday afternoon when Chris was ten, something on the TV changed everything. Russ was watching a golf game, his favorite weekend pastime. Chris was utterly enchanted. He couldn't keep his eyes off the winsomely mischievous player wearing jaunty yellow knickers, high argyle socks, and a Scottish tam o' shanter cap. The golfer's name was Payne Stewart.

Chris adored everything about him. We didn't know Payne personally, of course, but it felt like we did. It was as if Payne himself came right through that TV set. When Chris said, "Mom, I want me a pair of those yellow pants-things," I headed straight for the fabric store and my trusty Singer. Sewed him a tam, too. Chris couldn't wait to try them on, vowing to have a career in golf himself. Just like Payne Stewart.

It was the closest thing to hope we'd felt since that dreadful March morning.

Chris wrote a letter to Payne Stewart, enclosing a photo of himself wearing the knickers I'd sewn. "Now, don't get your hopes up, Son," I warned Chris. "Athletes are busy, busy, busy. I'm sure he gets lots of letters."

Chris simply believed. And when he got a return letter from Payne inviting Chris to visit his home, Chris just grinned like he'd known all along it would happen.

We made that trip to visit Payne. He treated us like family. I still have to pinch myself at what happened next. This legendary athlete who went on to be a member of the U.S. Ryder Cup team, to win two U.S. Opens and eleven PGA Tours, to become the world's eighth-ranked professional golfer, and more? Took our son under his wing.

We began to travel all over the country to watch his tournaments, and he introduced Chris to other pro golfers. Once he let Chris caddy nine holes for him. At other times he gifted Chris with personal treasures, like the club from his 1991 U.S. Open win. Throughout all the years of Chris's treatment, he kept our hope alive that Chris would not only live, but live the stuff of dreams. And when Chris graduated, cancer-free, from high school, Payne delivered the commencement address via video.

Throughout all the years of Chris's treatment, he kept our hope alive that Chris would not only live, but live the stuff of dreams.

On October 25, 1999, Chris and I were in Payne's home office with his secretary, admiring the trophy Payne had won when his final putt claimed the U.S. Open, when news came that sent shockwaves through our souls and seismic waves all over the world. The small jet Payne had chartered had crashed.

We later learned that everyone aboard lost their life. One of the few things that survived was the black nylon bracelet Payne had been wearing. It was inscribed with WWJD—*What Would Jesus Do?* That question explained his extravagant, giving heart that stretched to include an ordinary family from a little town in West Virginia. And countless others.

For years we mourned Payne Stewart as a family. We struggled with questions of why such a good person was taken, at just 42 years of age, when so many people needed him.

Payne's influence lived on in Chris, who went on in 2010 to embark on a career as a PGA golf professional, working as a master golf fitter and master club builder, teaching others the game. But it took a special connection for us to realize just how many lives Payne Stewart had touched.

While on Facebook recently, I stumbled upon a song. The words and melody reached deep into my soul. "Could you Google it?" I asked Randy Davis, the music director at my church who can learn anything. "Play it for me?" He did just that, and I loved it even more.

I researched the song's origin. A chill ran up and down my spine at what I discovered. A man by the name of Clint Brown had written it out of his own admiration for Payne Stewart. It was a response to Clint's questions about Payne's tragic death—questions that echoed my family's—and the answers God had given Clint.

The song tells of God's boundless grace protecting us from the things we can't see, sheltering us from life's storms, shielding us: "A hopeless case, an empty place / If not for Grace." I believe the song is part of God's plan, that Clint wrote it for me and for everyone who had been touched by Payne Stewart's love.

One day, as Chris was at home during a day off, he looked up from his computer. "You won't believe this, Mom. Clint Brown is going to be singing at a church in Kentucky." I'd always wanted to hear him, but he'd never been this close before.

We headed out down I-64 for Frenchburg, Kentucky. Took the Morehead exit, then the backroads, making a left at the IGA, then up a holler to Bethel Baptist, where a crowd had gathered for the outdoor evening service. It had a camp meeting feel like days of old. We were so excited that we told our story to some of the church workers who were helping to organize the event, letting them know how much it meant to us to be there.

When Clint settled in at the keyboard and looked out over the audience, it was exactly as I'd imagined. A balmy breeze enveloped me, as comforting as the Holy Spirit I knew was there. God sent Payne Stewart to us in our pain years ago, and Clint's song to me to answer the lingering questions in my heart.

God sent Payne Stewart to us in our pain years ago, and Clint's song to me to answer the lingering questions in my heart.

My eyes took in the musician with the dark, curly hair, the beckoning smile. "I understand I have some friends here from West Virginia," Clint said warmly. Then the words and melody my heart had longed for without knowing what it needed. A story that told *my* story, *our* story—the story of every one of us touched by the grace that finds us when and where we need it, that refuses to leave us in a dark, hopeless place. Grace we can't be good enough to ever earn, nor bad enough to ever lose. God's gift that is offered to us all. I sang the lyrics along with Clint as I had a thousand times before: "A hopeless case, an empty place / If not for grace."

Payne loved the game of golf, but it had been a vehicle for loving people. For him, grace was no cliché, but the ultimate trophy. Our hero now lived in heaven, as does my life partner and Chris's father. My spirit brimmed with blessings. These two men who had meant the world to us had been made for another world, the Place of Grace with the Giver of that grace. When our earthly sojourn is complete, my son and I will join them.

Until then there's a tender place in my heart reserved just for them. The memories soothe my soul, but they can never fill it. That place is reserved for grace alone. It is anything but empty.

The Place I Most Wanted to See

Marlene Kropf

Of all the showings revealed to me, the one that gave me the most comfort was that our sweet Lord—who is infinitely exalted and alone is worthy of worship— is also utterly simple and friendly.

—Julian of Norwich

It was my first day in the British Isles. After enjoying a full cooked English breakfast—bacon, eggs, fried tomato and mushrooms with toast and marmalade—my husband and I set out to find the place in England I most wanted to visit: the cell where Julian of Norwich lived in spiritual retreat and seclusion from the world.

The one surviving book we have of Julian's, *Revelations of Divine Love*, was written more than 600 years ago and is known as the first book written by a woman in English. After she survived a severe illness at age thirty, Julian wrote about visions of the crucified Jesus that she received as she lay near death. The warmth and intimacy of her conversations with Jesus moved me; she often referred to Jesus as "friendly" or as her "courteous Lord." My own images of

God, which had tended to be distant and demanding, were slowly transformed as I pondered her visions. Because of her insights and influence, I claimed Julian as my spiritual mother. Julian's cell, the enclosure where she spent a cloistered life in communion with God, was at the top of my list of places to visit.

All through that first day of travel, my husband and I stopped frequently to admire and take photos of gardens, quaint cottages, and village churches. By the time we reached the bustling city of Norwich, it was already late in the day. In that era before internet communication, I hadn't been able to find the exact address of Julian's cell, so we drove to Norwich Cathedral, hoping someone there could direct us.

The soothing chants of evensong greeted us as we entered the cathedral. While waiting in the narthex, we looked for a brochure or other information about Julian's cell but found nothing. At last the service concluded, and worshippers began streaming out of the sanctuary. A sister in a traditional black habit noticed our bewilderment and approached us. "What are you looking for?" she asked. When I told her, she responded, "It's almost closing time. Follow me!"

Our guide sprinted through the twisting city streets and rush-hour traffic with us in tow, hurrying to keep pace. Eventually she stopped short in an alley, looking puzzled. "The street sign is missing!" she exclaimed. "But here is the lane to the church."

A few moments later, we entered the church and noticed a sign posted on a side door: "Mother Julian's Cell." I breathed a sigh of relief and followed our guide through the arched doorway.

Inside, in the quiet peace of early evening, the rector of the church was meditating in solitude. "You need to leave," our guide said briskly. "These folks have come a long way to visit Julian's cell."

Without a word, he smiled and walked away. When I turned to thank the sister, I discovered she had disappeared.

Our guide sprinted through the twisting city streets and rush-hour traffic with us in tow, hurrying to keep pace.

She was nowhere to be seen! *Strange,* I thought. But I turned my attention immediately to the cell.

It was a small space, about 10 feet square. Within this humble enclosure, Julian had lived out her vows as an anchorite, devoting herself so completely to her religious practice that she never left the room. Most of her time was spent in prayer and quiet meditation. A window on one wall opened into the sanctuary, where she would have been able to hear and watch the daily prayer services of the congregation and receive communion on Sundays. Another window opened onto what would have been a busy street in Julian's day (now a quiet garden). During certain hours, Julian opened her window and was available to offer spiritual counsel to passers-by who requested it.

As I lit a candle and breathed in the holiness of the cell, Julian's words, written on my heart, reverberated in the solitude. "It is a source of endless joy, bliss, and delight to me that I suffered for you," Jesus spoke to her. In a vibrant image, she described the gift of salvation as a fine garment: "Our Savior turned Adam's old tunic—tight, threadbare, and short, into a gleaming garment—fresh and beautiful, white and bright. He was clothed anew in everlasting purity."

I had been given a wondrous and amazing gift—a fulfillment of my heart's desire.

In her visions, Julian heard God's reassuring voice: "See my hand in all my works: I shall never lift it, for all eternity. See, I guide all things to the goal I ordained for them, by the same power, wisdom, and love with which I created them. How could anything possibly be amiss?" In response, she affirmed that "God is our clothing; he wraps himself around us, enfolding us in his love. His tender love is our shelter; he will never leave us."

Perhaps the best known of the messages Julian received is a powerful, repeated affirmation: "I shall make all things well. You will see for yourself: every kind of thing shall be well." I too felt the Spirit's reassuring presence as I lingered in the silence of her cell.

Finally, it was closing time. The rector came to lock the church, and my husband and I reluctantly departed. But as we walked back to Norwich Cathedral, where our car was parked, my thoughts went back to the mysterious woman who had guided us to the cell. If she hadn't noticed our perplexity, or if she had simply tried to give us verbal directions, we never would have found the cell because of the missing signpost at the end of the lane. After all my years of longing to visit the cell, I could have departed, keenly disappointed. Instead, I had been given a wondrous and amazing gift—a fulfillment of my heart's desire.

Might she have been an angel? If not a miraculous presence, then certainly someone who listened attentively to the Spirit's nudges.

At the end of my first day in the British Isles, I vowed I would return to Norwich, but the next time I would stay longer. The love that had lured me across an ocean to my spiritual mother's home had awakened a yearning to comprehend Julian's visions more fully and to claim the wisdom that had grounded and guided her: "Love is my Lord's meaning."

And if there were a next time, I hoped I would have an opportunity to thank the mysterious guide who had led us to Julian's cell in the first place.

Note: A fine contemporary translation of Julian's medieval text is *The Showings of Julian of Norwich* by Mirabai Starr (Hampton Roads Publishing Company, 2013).

The French Grocery Store Miracle

Mary DeMuth

By faith he made his home in the promised land like a stranger in a foreign country.
—Hebrews 11:9 (NIV)

When we lived in France as church planters in the early 2000s, my least favorite errand was grocery shopping. The aisles loomed narrow; the people didn't seem to operate with the same courtesy I'd known stateside; and you constantly had to rein in a grocery cart whose wheels were not fixed, so you had to maneuver it sideways, being careful not to hit an errant French child. When we returned from serving overseas, I often rejoiced at the ease of US grocery stores.

My husband, Patrick, and I had only been back to southern France once before we took a mission team from our church to visit the work we had started so many years prior. It had been 14 years between leaving France and this new adventure. In that hiccup of time, I'd written dozens of books.

My heart felt uneasy as we planned the trip. Much of what happened on the soil of southern France had been traumatic, and I feared falling into the vortex of depression. Still, we pressed forward to lead this small team in the fall of 2021.

Prior to coming, I led a writer's intensive in Switzerland for two groups of writers, for one week each. Those weeks had drained me, and, at that moment in my writing career, I'd been weathering quite a lot of bad publishing news. I felt small, unnoticed, and discouraged at the current lackluster state of my writing journey. Part of me wanted to bypass France and just come home.

In light of that, I'd sent my email list a quick update, asking for prayer. I let them know I'd be in Switzerland, then in southern France, particularly Grasse, the perfume capital of France.

Our team landed on a Sunday, when all the grocery stores are closed, which meant we would not be able to navigate those scary aisles. So on Monday morning, in need of food for the week, we debated which grocery store to visit. Though there were several to choose from, my husband and I settled on E. LeClerc in the valley below us because it had always been our favorite, most easily navigated French grocery store.

I assigned tasks to each team member—pick up yogurt, meat, cheese (of course!), drinks, and snacks. I hoped they'd be able to figure out where things were. Imagine the team's surprise when they found out there was an entire refrigerator aisle of yogurt! Another one was dedicated to chocolate. Several aisles boasted all sorts of French cheeses and cold cuts. I spoke to the team in English, while simultaneously asking grocers where items were in French.

This was during the Covid pandemic, so I wore a mask during all this grocery directing. As I stood at the end of the yogurt aisle, I noticed a woman (also masked) looking at me. She approached me and asked—in English, with no trace of a French accent—"Excuse me, are you Mary DeMuth?"

I didn't know what to say. For several seconds, I couldn't say a thing! Then, a team member next to me said, "Yes, she's Mary!"

"I am Sonia," the woman told me. "I receive your emails." She then went on to say she'd subscribed a few years ago, and noticed that I would be in Grasse, close to where she lived. "I had prayed, 'Lord, if it's possible, would you please let me meet Mary?'"

"Oh my goodness!" I choked back tears.

"And then this morning, I had to drop my daughter off at school, and I figured I'd stop at the grocery store. I typically don't go to this one, but I felt somehow that I should. And here you are!"

By now we were making an emotional scene in the yogurt aisle, but I didn't care. We decided that our team would go have tea with her later in the week.

When we arrived at her house, she shared a bit of her life, and we had the privilege of listening to her story and praying for her. We worshipped together as she detailed her loneliness in France, her need for friends, and her desire to see her child follow Jesus. Sonia was Canadian, married to a French man, and longed for fellowship with other believers.

I had the privilege of introducing her to other Christ followers very near her home, and we all marveled at this surprising "coincidence" of us all being in this random French grocery store at just the right time, and her recognizing me even through a mask.

But what came next revealed just how sweet God is to us. She told me as we were leaving, "What you do matters. Don't stop writing. Your ministry is important." It's exactly what I needed to hear after my deep discouragement. I realized God saw me. He had used my words in Sonia's life, then supernaturally orchestrated our meeting so that Sonia would be encouraged that He answers prayer, and to show me that He took note of my discouragement. And all this in one of the most stressful places I'd remembered from our time as missionaries —a grocery store.

There was one last bit of icing on the cake. Sonia relayed the crazy story to her child, who had been doubting God of late. After hearing it, the child said, "God is really real!"

God's Mysterious Ways: Chance Meetings

One of God's favorite ways to connect with us is to put someone in our path who can give us an answer to a question or a word of encouragement just when we need it. In the stories you just read, we saw some travelers encounter a nun who guided them to a holy site, and an author meeting someone inspired by her work at a time when they both needed it.

Who might you encounter today who can point you where you need to go? Or might you be in the right place to help someone or lift them up? Here are some steps you can take to explore that idea further.

- **Pray.** If you find yourself with a problem, and you're not sure what to do, talk to God about it. Ask Him to send someone who can help you find a solution.

- **Seek.** Pay attention to the people who cross your path, whether through a planned meeting or a chance encounter. Might one of them be able to offer some insight?

- **Act.** If you get a nudge from God to go somewhere you hadn't planned to go, or talk to someone you might have otherwise passed by, follow that nudge.

- **Reflect.** Might there have been times when you were the one who was put in a certain place and time to help another person? Maybe a meeting that seemed like a crazy coincidence? Could it have been God at work?

More Prayer, More Power!

Joe Fletcher

*Acknowledge him in all your ways, and
he will make your paths straight.*
—Proverbs 3:6 (NET)

I was 25 years old and naïve enough to think that I was ready to plant and pastor a church in the Bronx, New York. I left Bible college and graduate school with a good background in Scripture and theology. I learned public speaking and how to organize a sermon. But Bible college did not teach me everything. It didn't teach me what to do when an intoxicated woman interrupts a church service. It didn't teach me how to raise money for a church that was in one of the poorest congressional districts in the country. And it didn't teach me how to locate and purchase a church building in the Bronx.

Like most startup churches in the inner city, we initially rented a small storefront. That was a reasonable place to begin. But as our little church began to grow, it was clear that renting was not a good long-term plan. Our storefront was small, so it would limit our growth. Our landlord raised our rent at every opportunity. And since New Yorkers don't always take storefront churches seriously, we lacked credibility. We needed our own church building, and I was determined to make this happen.

In most parts of the country, the conventional way to get a church building is to purchase a plot of land and simply build. This strategy will rarely work in the Bronx. First, it is very unusual, if not impossible, to find vacant land of any size. Almost every bit of land in the Bronx already has some sort of structure built on it. Secondly, vacant land is very expensive. Just one acre would cost millions.

But I knew what our church needed, and I was determined to find it. Maybe we could find an existing church building that was for sale. That would be ideal, but unlikely. Maybe we could find some sort of warehouse that we could convert into a church building. I was sure that the Lord would open some door for us. I wrote letters, checked ads, and connected with real estate brokers. I even knocked on doors of random buildings hoping to find the right fit.

After more than 2 years in our initial storefront, I found the answer—at least I thought I had. It was a commercial building with a store that we could convert into a sanctuary. As the store was a bit larger than our first storefront, it allowed for some growth. It even had a couple of apartments upstairs that we could rent out to help offset the expenses. We could use the basement for youth and nursery. This was a rather unconventional move, and it certainly wasn't ideal. But it was clearly an upgrade from our first location. So we made a plan. We would initially rent this building. That would give us time to raise funds and find a lender. From there, we had the option to purchase the building. But sadly, we just couldn't get funding. So we rented this space until we could find a more permanent solution.

Then the answer came—at least I thought it had. It was a large warehouse on East Tremont Avenue, a main hub in the Bronx. I met with the retiring owner. He was what we call "old school." He simply sized me up and decided to work with me. Our members scraped together $10,000 as an up-front payment.

But I knew what our church needed, and I was determined to find it.

We would rent from him for a certain term. At the end of that term, we would purchase the building for $500,000. We would give him $90,000 as a down payment, and he would hold the mortgage for the balance owed.

We moved into this warehouse full of hope. The building was a gigantic 16,000 square feet. This would give us room to grow for decades. And since we certainly didn't need all of that space initially, we could rent out the parts that we weren't using. That would make it possible for us to pay our huge monthly rent. But it was difficult. Finding and keeping good tenants was a constant struggle. This produced financial pressure that prevented us from having any money left over to upgrade the building. It also left no margin in our budget to begin saving up for the $90,000 down payment that we would eventually need when it was time to purchase the building. And maybe worst of all, we had a constant problem with rats—big rats—South Bronx rats! In short, I had gotten us in over our heads. We finally realized this and moved out.

Shortly after we moved out of the warehouse, we connected with a church only a block away. Their once-vibrant congregation was now down to five people. As they had practically no income, they were looking for a church to rent their building for services. I met with one of their leaders. I agreed to rent from them, as long as there was a clear understanding that, within a year or two, our church would purchase the building. Their church also owned a parsonage. We agreed on a price of $150,000 for both. I had finally gotten us into a position where our congregation would have its own building—at least I thought I had!

The building was about a hundred years old when we began renting. It needed some serious repair. One of our jokes was, "When it rains outside, it also rains inside." Not funny! But I kept encouraging myself and our members with the thought that, since we were getting such a good deal on the two structures, we could work together and repair everything once we owned them. We were there for about a year when their lawyer began drawing up the contract of sale. Then came the phone call. Their board had changed the terms of the sale. They now wanted $250,000 for the church and parsonage! What was once a good deal was now a very bad deal. It was a deal that no reasonable person would agree to. Within three weeks, we had moved out. Thankfully, I was friends with the pastor of a nearby Spanish-speaking church. He graciously let us rent their church building on Sunday afternoons.

By this time, I was not in a good place personally. I began to doubt myself. If God wanted us to have our own building, why couldn't we achieve this?

Just a few months after we began renting the building from the Spanish-speaking church, I met with our church members and told them: "For years I have tried everything to figure out how to get us the right building. I have failed. I am asking all of us to take the next week and pray for God's direction. No brokers. No ads. No cold calls. We are just going to pray."

Our church family prayed that week. All of our prayers focused on one request: "Lord, show us the building You want us to purchase!" We were hoping and praying for an answer that week. But by Friday, there seemed to be no answer in sight.

> *"I am asking all of us to take the next week and pray for God's direction. No brokers. No ads. No cold calls. We are just going to pray."*

Saturday, in a shopping area near where our church was meeting, we were passing out flyers and inviting people to services. I struck up a brief conversation with a complete stranger. As she was leaving, she turned back and said, "Could you please pray for our church? We have a building that we need to sell!"

I drove by the church building that afternoon. I contacted the pastor of that church that evening. By Monday, our members had unanimously agreed to purchase this building. I had finally found the place that I believed God wanted for us. And this time, I was right! Eighteen years after our first service in our tiny storefront, we finally moved into our own building.

And everyone in our church knew that the hand of God had brought us there.

It's not that we had never asked for God's direction until that week of prayer. We had. But there is a difference between praying casually and praying with intense purpose. There is a difference between praying for general guidance, and praying like the result depends entirely on God. And the outcome was a "coincidental" meeting that otherwise might never have happened.

Twenty years after we purchased the building, I retired. It was a privilege to pass the baton of leadership to a great—and younger—man of God. Infinity Bible Church continues to preach the Gospel of Jesus Christ and make an impact for His Kingdom from that same building. Its youth program and after-school program have impacted hundreds of young lives. Its food pantry continues to demonstrate the love of Christ in a tangible way by feeding hundreds of needy families each month.

Now, the members of Infinity Bible Church have another problem. Their building is just too small!

A Car, a Wedding, and a Post

Ashley Kappel

And this is what he promised us—eternal life.
—1 John 2:25 (NIV)

The sun had finally set on our wedding day. Brian and I had danced, toasted, vowed, and feasted with dozens of our favorite people and were just about to head to the car when my dad pulled us aside. "I'm really sorry," he said. "But I was backing your car up today and I dented the bumper. I promise I'll fix it."

Here's what you need to know about my dad. An orthopedic surgeon in a small town, he accepted corn as payment when the years were lean. He attended every sporting event any of his four children participated in, often driving across the state with my mom late into the night to be there. He lived to brag about our modest accomplishments. He never broke his promises to us. He had always provided everything we needed, so I had no concerns about him fixing the car, but many concerns that he was worried about it on a day of celebration.

"I'm not worried about it," I told him. "I promise! And I don't want you to worry about it either." I hugged him and waved goodbye as Brian and I hopped in the slightly worse-for-wear car and drove off into the night.

The next morning, Brian and I surveyed the damage. A low parking lot post had been the culprit, popping in the corner of the rear bumper and smashing the taillight. Easily fixable, but not worth dealing with before the honeymoon. We assured my dad we would fix the damage when we got back and headed off for a week of sandy beaches and slow sunsets.

The day after we got back, I got the call. My dad, a mountain of a man in my life, had died. Suddenly, unexpectedly—all these words that I thought I understood now swam through the phone as I struggled to figure out what was going on.

The next week was a whirlwind. I ended up in my hometown planning a funeral alongside my mom. My car sat hours away at my in-laws' house, waiting for me to start the life I was supposed to be living.

After the service on our way back home, we called my in-laws, who were ready to do anything to help right our newly upended world. "I got in touch with a local body shop and when they asked me to send a picture of the damage, I went out and, well," she said, pausing on the line. "Ashley, the dent isn't there. It's gone."

When we finally arrived at home, we pulled into the driveway and walked straight to my car. Sure enough, the taillight still boasted jagged, cracked edges, but the dent, like my mother-in-law had said, had vanished.

"It was really there, right?" Brian and I asked each other. "Are we nuts?"

For the next 5 years, I drove that car with the taillight busted—a constant reminder that I wasn't crazy. There had been a dent there. Perhaps it had been righted by the Alabama heat—or maybe it was one last gift from Dad on his way out of the world. My heart still ached, but he'd left me with the reassurance that a father's promise endures.

Where He Guides

Renee Mitchell

The LORD will guide you continually, and satisfy your soul in drought, and strengthen your bones; you shall be like a watered garden, and like a spring of water, whose waters do not fail.
—Isaiah 58:11 (NKJV)

Sitting in our truck in the parking lot of Central Bible College in Springfield, Missouri, I bowed my head to pray. It was a beautiful July day, and a few minutes earlier my husband, Larry, had kissed my cheek and told me it was all going to work out. "Where God guides, He provides," he'd said as he exited the vehicle. I was too worried for my husband's words to really sink in. I needed to get to God and ask Him what our next step was.

We had dropped absolutely everything to move to Missouri so that my husband could finish Bible college. When he had originally applied to the college and put in for a transfer to a place closer to the school, we weren't sure when it would be approved. We thought maybe he would get the transfer in a couple of months and then start classes in the spring. But then a transfer opportunity came up more quickly than expected, and he was accepted to the college for the fall semester.

Everything fell into place—with only two weeks until fall classes were to begin. My head was still reeling from all the changes: the move, quitting our jobs, dragging our children to another state away from their church, friends—and, more importantly, family. It had not been an easy task. It had felt as if I'd had my heart ripped out and then purposely ripped out theirs. I was angry, and scared, and wishing I was anywhere else, doing anything else. But the move was done, and now it was time to settle in.

I was angry, and scared, and wishing I was anywhere else, doing anything else. But the move was done, and now it was time to settle in.

While Larry was in the admissions office registering and getting books taken care of, I sat in the parking lot with my head in my hands, asking the Lord for a miracle. I needed to find a job as soon as possible to help support the family financially. My husband would be working full-time while taking classes. I knew that meant I wouldn't see him much, so I had put in some applications for jobs on campus, hoping to be closer to him. So far, there had been no response.

I was tired, having been so busy and so worried about the future that I hadn't slept in days. We had been cleaning and moving, and I looked horrible. My hair was up in a bun and I had no makeup on. But I wanted to get out of the truck and stretch my legs, so I wandered into the administration building to use the restroom and get a drink of water.

As I entered, there was a woman sitting at a receptionist desk. I will never forget her beautiful smile. "Hello," she said pleasantly. "Can I help you?"

"I'm looking for the restroom," I explained.

She struck up a conversation, asking me my name and what brought me to the college. I don't know what came over me, but when I opened my mouth, everything poured out. I explained that we had just moved there and that I was looking for a job. I told her that I was a secretary and practically went through my résumé. I even told her about the situation with my husband. I couldn't believe I was so open with a complete stranger, but she was so easy to talk to, and I guess I needed someone to listen. She pointed out the restroom to me. As I walked away, I noticed that another young woman came and relieved her of her duties. It was around lunchtime, so I figured she was stepping away.

A few days went by, and I spent most of my time getting the kids and Larry settled in. I homeschooled my two teens, and they worked in the evenings. They had both been blessed to get jobs pretty quickly. I was the one who seemed to be waiting.

One day as I was gathering the laundry, my phone rang. I had an interview at Central Bible College the next morning! It was for the role of campus employment coordinator. I had no idea what that was, but I was going to put on my best dress and make the greatest impression I could.

I prayed all night. Isaiah 58:11 kept running through my mind: "The Lord will guide you always; he will satisfy your needs in a sun-scorched land and will strengthen your frame. You will be like a well-watered garden, like a spring whose waters never fail" (NIV).

I walked into the administration building and to that same receptionist desk. There was someone else sitting there, and she gave me directions to Human Resources. As I entered the room, there sat the lady with the beautiful smile from weeks before, behind a nameplate that said "Rhoda" and "Human Resources Director"!

"I liked your application and your résumé," she told me, her hands clasped together. "And your honesty when we first met was refreshing."

I could have passed out. I remember well what I had looked like and how I rambled on and on about why we were there and how I was trusting God to provide.

She hired me on the spot. I got to work side by side with her for 5 years and I loved it! She was everything a supervisor should be. She was kind and smart and truly one of the best Christian women I have ever met. She taught me what it means to be a woman of God.

Many times we talked about that first day we met. She always said I had a glow about me when I walked in. I knew it was the precious spirit of God. He had been with me, and He led me straight to her.

As I walked out of that admin building the day I was hired, I smiled. God always provides where He guides.

Beyond a Pocket-Dial

Celeste Huttes

*Look for the little hints of magic glittering
at the corners of your life.*
—Martha Beck

My heart was heavy as I set off on a solitary walk at the park I frequented with Dixie, my sweet (and occasionally stubborn) Cairn Terrier mix. After just two precious years together, it had become clear that Dixie's days were coming to an end.

The odds were against her when I adopted her. Not only was she 10 years old at the time, but she carried excess weight that had created some health issues.

Still, the zest for life displayed by this sweet and spunky senior never failed to inspire me. The way she would "gallop" on our walks, in spite of her robust size, tickled me every time. While her body failed, her spirit soared.

On that June day, the vet wanted to keep Dixie to administer fluids and make her more comfortable. I went for a walk to try to clear my mind—and quickly learned that nothing is lonelier than a walk without your best friend by your side.

At the park, I ran into a former coworker I tried to put on a happy face during our brief visit, not wanting to fall apart if he happened to ask where my dog was. After we parted ways, I began to think about my friend Diana, who used to work for this man. Diana had moved out of state after retiring, and I missed her presence in my life.

From the moment we met, Diana felt like a kindred spirit to me. Warm, witty, and nurturing, she was a source of comfort when times were tough. Still, I have never been one to pick up the phone when I'm feeling down. Sometimes, I just need to sit with the sadness—which is exactly what I was doing that day in the park.

As I continued my walk, Diana popped into my mind several times. And then—out of the blue—I heard "Hello?" coming from behind me. My jeans pocket, to be specific. To my surprise and delight, I had somehow "pocket-dialed" Diana!

After a brief chat and plans to reconnect soon, I went on my way, lighter than before.

Of all the names and numbers in my phone, it was Diana's voice I heard at the very moment I was thinking of her, and exactly when I needed a boost.

This amazing little "God-incidence" brightened my day and reminded me that those I love—from Diana to Dixie—are only a thought away.

Tired Tents

David Wylie

Let us not become weary in doing good, for at the proper time we will reap a harvest if we do not give up.

—Galatians 6:9 (NIV)

I had just sat down in my chair with a hot cup of coffee. Peace and quiet. After a full career as a highway patrolman and deputy sheriff, I was more than tired, I was flat-out exhausted. Don't get me wrong, I loved my career and all that came with it, including the crazy schedule and long hours. But it felt nice to start my day with a cup of coffee that wasn't served in a Styrofoam cup through a drive-up window.

I also enjoyed my quiet time with the Lord as the sun cast a rosy glow in the sky. That hadn't always been easy to fit in, especially when I was on call.

Briing. Briiing. The phone interrupted my thoughts. I looked at my watch. It was only 6:15 in the morning. I was used to phone calls anytime of the day or night all the years I was working but hoped that my "on call" days were behind me.

"For Pete's sake!" I muttered as I moved my Bible and daily devotion to the side. *Lord, You know I am retired! I have put in my time and am ready for a rest.*

Recognizing the number that flashed across the screen, I answered the phone.

"Hello?" I tried to sound more enthusiastic than I felt at the time.

The friend on the other end apologized for the early call, but, knowing the hours I had kept for decades, he knew I would be up. Then he cut to the point of his call. "I would like for you to come out to see some property I am thinking about

I tried to focus on what my friend was saying, but the nudging continued, as if the Lord was trying to get up into my business.

buying. Let's meet at the Waffle House in the middle of town and I'll spring for breakfast."

"Well," I responded, "that sounds fine. I was fixin' to have breakfast soon, so I'll just meet you there in about forty-five minutes."

Lately it seemed that I was busier in retirement than I had been when I worked full time. I pulled my boots on, grabbed my keys, and let my wife, Ann, know I would be having breakfast with a friend in town.

Sure enough, when I pulled into the parking lot, I saw my friend next to his car. The morning rush was already starting to fill up the restaurant, but we didn't wait long before we were seated and our orders were placed. Our server, a young man I had never seen before, quickly brought out our coffees while we waited.

My friend began to tell me about the property he was looking at purchasing and some of the things he had been working on. While he spoke, I started to feel this little nudging. I tried to focus on what my friend was saying, but the nudging continued, as if the Lord was trying to get up into my business. Only this business was not about giving advice to my friend about property. This business hit a little closer to home—in fact, it was as close as the back pocket where I kept my wallet.

Lord, I am tired and retired! Can't you get someone else to do whatever needs done? But I felt the Lord pushing me to take action. I reached into my back pocket and pulled out my well-worn leather wallet, knowing that I had a hundred-dollar bill inside, just in case I needed it.

When the young man came to the table with our food, I knew what the Lord wanted me to do.

"Son," I looked up at him as he slipped the plates of waffles, eggs, and sausage in front of us. "I have no idea what is going on in your life, but the Lord has really impressed on me that you might need this more than I do." I handed him the folded bill. Without a word the young man slipped the bill into his apron pocket, turned, and walked away.

OK, Lord, I guess that's it, I thought as I watched him step into the kitchen through the swinging door.

My friend and I talked as we ate. We were just about finished when the young man came back to our table. He looked like he had been crying.

"Sir," he said. "You couldn't have known this, but I am trying to get back on my feet and I really need this job. My old car that I need to get to work just broke down. The mechanic said it was going to be an easy fix, but without any extra cash I wasn't sure what I was going to do. The parts to fix my car cost a hundred dollars."

I nodded, and replied, "Well, I couldn't have known that, but the Lord sure did."

My friend paid our tabs, and as soon we were finished looking over the property I headed back home.

When I got to the house Ann had already left for the afternoon. I pulled off my boots and sat back down in my easy chair. Finally, peace and a quiet place to rest, right where I had been when the phone rang. I picked up the small daily devotional I kept near my Bible and opened it to that day's reading.

I stifled a chuckle when I saw the title at the top, in bold letters: "Tired Tents."

I would have missed out on helping that young man if I had decided I was too tired to answer that early-morning phone call.

God has such a sense of humor. Just because I had the plaque on my wall that said I was no longer part of the Highway Patrol Service did not mean I was out of God's service.

God's Mysterious Ways: Is God Trying to Tell You Something?

Sometimes when God speaks, it's through a little nudge to do this thing or that thing. Sometimes it's through a sign, a too-perfect-to-be-coincidence object that catches your notice, or a song when you didn't expect it. Sometimes it's a call from a friend—or a call you accidentally made yourself!

What are the ways that God talks to you? They may not be as obvious as the examples in these pages, but here are some ways you can explore that idea:

- **Pray.** Ask God if He's been trying to talk to you. Was there a sign that you missed? Do you want Him to "speak" to you more? Let Him know your questions, and listen for the answers. If you like, try asking Him for a specific type of object (a flower, for example) as your special sign.

- **Seek.** Keep an eye out as you go about your day for signs that God is speaking to you. If you find yourself getting busy, don't forget to slow down occasionally and be alert to what's happening around you.

- **Act.** If you see (or hear, or smell, or feel) your sign, say "thank You" to God right then and there.

- **Reflect.** Are there times in the past when you've received signs from God? What was He saying? Did you understand it at the time, or did you only realize what happened later?

A Love Note Named Brooke

Dee Dee Parker

*Whether you turn to the right or to the left,
your ears will hear a voice behind you, saying,
"This is the way; walk in it."*

—Isaiah 30:21 (NIV)

Fall in my daughter Brooke's neighborhood was always special, with homes sporting pots of mums and bright orange pumpkins. But even in the midst of all those colors, Brooke's home stood out. Her husband marveled at how many plastic bins holding stems of silk leaves, pumpkin spice candles, and pumpkins of all sizes and shapes one person could gather. The bounty of bins grew every year until stacks filled a corner of the garage. My daughter loved fall and decorating for Halloween.

Several years before, Brooke had been diagnosed with cancer. I moved in with her to be her caregiver. Many hospital stays and treatments ensued, but Brooke bravely fought on. In the midst of her suffering, she always thought of others. She started a ministry of giving precious hand-crocheted soft hats to patients taking chemo. This ministry was named Brooke's

Bonnets. She loved to give her bonnets to children suffering the effects of the harsh treatments.

I had carried the decorations into the house that year. I made new ribbons for wreaths, arranged centerpieces on tabletops, and hung garlands from the fireplace mantel. Outside of Brooke's large picture window, trees displayed their fall wardrobe in vibrant reds, greens, and orange.

I then attacked the front and back doors and both porches. Brooke wanted the children to be greeted with happy fall decorations—nothing scary was allowed. She loved dressing up and handing out candy to the throngs of children coming from all over town. The parents and children knew it was a loving place to trick-or-treat.

This was the first year Brooke would not be waiting at the door with specially made goodie bags to distribute amid the calls of "Trick or treat!" During the months leading up to this particular Halloween, Brooke's illness progressed, but in true Brooke fashion, she thought of a way she could participate in the joy of the night. Since she was confined to a hospital bed, she decided her costume would be that of a mummy. We wrapped her with bandages to dress rehearse for Halloween. She wanted to give out candy from her hospital bed and not scare the kids.

But Brooke didn't get to use her last bit of creativity; she died the day before Halloween.

Her husband and I were devastated. Our precious daughter and beloved wife had left us. We knew she was in heaven, not suffering, but it was so hard to say goodbye.

Halloween rolled around and we couldn't bear to turn on the porch lights, or any other lights. Just the day before, I had walked behind her hearse out of the neighborhood, streets lined with neighbors saying goodbye to Brooke. We were grieving and couldn't greet throngs of happy children.

Yet, wanting to honor her and find a small measure of comfort in that time of loss, I decided to leave her home at dusk and hand out candy to one child, a "Brooke treat" to honor the daughter I'd lost.

Desperately wanting to make a meaningful connection, I asked God to lead me to the right child. I wandered amid the throngs of children for some time, trying to keep it together. Joy filled the air for the children. Brooke always loved that, as did I, but this was a challenging task: a moment

---

I decided to leave her home at dusk and hand out candy to one child, a "Brooke treat" to honor the daughter I'd lost.

---

of self-sacrifice and honor, a moment of trusting God when I was broken.

Then I saw something. I felt my spirit quicken as I recognized who I was to give the special treat to. Down in a cul-de-sac like my daughter's sat a van. It was fairly quiet, without lots of trick-or-treaters. I didn't want to cry with children around.

Approaching the mom, who was standing outside a van holding a plastic pumpkin, I asked, "Don't you think you're a little old to be trick or treating?" We both chuckled.

Her sweet daughter sat in the seat near the open sliding door, eating a hamburger meal before setting out in search of candy treasures.

I asked her mom if I could give her daughter some candy and she said, "Yes, of course."

Looking at the young girl, I saw blue eyes and a face framed by blonde hair, just like my daughter's. I said, "Hi. What's your name?"

At that moment, God reached down and showed me He was right there, in my most broken moment.

Turning her head, the little girl smiled. "My name is Brooke."

Tears gushed uncontrollably. Brooke's mom comforted me as I told her what had happened.

Despite the pain, God reached out and told me how much He loved me. He used His amazing guidance to show me that He was there, walking with us as we said goodbye to our dear Brooke.

Only God could orchestrate that love note to us.

Full Circle

Danielle Germain, as told to Elsa Kok Colopy

A time to weep and a time to laugh, a time to mourn and a time to dance.

—Ecclesiastes 3:4 (NIV)

He was the kind of big brother every little sister hopes for . . . cool, funny, strong, sarcastic, but incredibly loyal.

I adored him.

Even though everyone tried to get on the inside with him, I was already there. I was his sister, and he took his job of protecting me seriously. When I was little and had a bad dream, I would sneak down the hallway, tiptoe quietly into his room and then over to his bed. Ever so carefully I would lift the covers and curl up beside him. Half asleep, he would throw a protective arm over me. I was safe.

When I was fourteen and Caleb was seventeen, we lost my grandfather in a sailing accident. My family had been on a vacation in Alaska, so as soon as we got word, we flew to Florida. We spent the week together with all of our cousins and said goodbye to a man who had been part of our world all our lives.

When we arrived back home in Texas a week later, my brother needed some time with his friends. A whole group from our church went bowling, and he was out late blowing off some steam. We lived outside of town and on his way home, my brother fell asleep. Just a few miles from our house, he fell asleep and ran headlong into a tree.

And just like that, Caleb was gone.

The police knocked on our door early that morning. The details ran together in a horrific haze. There'd been an accident. Fallen asleep. Tree. Didn't suffer.

But oh, how we did.

Caleb had died instantly and with him, so many other things were shattered.

Caleb was my best friend. Not only was he there for my childhood nightmares, as teenagers he was the one I went to with all my girl drama. He protected me from bullies, and he was the one I talked to late into the night about boys and school and life. Caleb was tall, athletic, cool. Everyone loved him, and now it felt like we were all lost without him. Adding to the complexity, my parents are pastors of a large church. They'd founded it in their home, and it had grown to nearly 8,000 members by that time. Since our family was in the spotlight, our grief was in the limelight as well. It felt like there were a thousand eyes watching how we were carrying the weight of our pain. I remember standing in the shower one morning and just doubling over as the pain hit with what felt like a physical force. I sobbed, my tears being washed away as quickly as they flowed. I hated this! What should have been my most carefree years were stripped from me. I felt like a mutant teenager, like life would never be the same. I would always be different, altered fundamentally in the wake of this loss.

I turned inward. I turned away from the grief. I gravitated to boys, alcohol, and drugs to numb the pain. As I tunneled into darkness, my parents grasped for the light. They funneled their grief into promoting Caleb's legacy. They poured their heart, influence, and passion into ensuring that Caleb was never forgotten, that what he couldn't accomplish in his short life would be seen to in his death. They created the Caleb Foundation, and with those funds they built a home

Fredelin was an orphan with big dreams. He was a quiet one, but not for lack of things to say.

in Botswana for babies who could no longer be with their parents, a school in Uganda, and a Caleb House as part of an orphanage in Haiti. With the outpouring of love and resources from the community of Austin, hope was built around the world.

My addictions did nothing to heal me, and I ultimately landed in rehab to work through my heartbreak. While the pain still swept in like a thunderstorm on a warm summer's eve, I was better able to give in to it, to give it space, to cry when the tears came. I set aside the alcohol, the drugs, the boys. I leaned into my God and found ways to grieve in sobriety.

As the years passed, I longed to reconnect to Caleb in a healthy way. From this new place of healing, I wanted to tap into who he was, see his legacy, experience all that had come from his transition to heaven. I decided on a trip to Haiti, to the Caleb House, to get a glimpse of my brother again. I was 21 years old by this time, and I'll never forget seeing the Caleb House live and in person. His name, scrawled the way he used to sign it, on a building that now housed young men in transition. These guys were there to gain an education, learn a trade, and ultimately pour back into their home communities. Some of them would be able to come to America to gain an education. Their futures were bright.

Fredelin was one of those young men, an orphan with big dreams. He was a quiet one, but not for lack of things to say. His story had its own hard places, and he was now staying at the Caleb House to build a future. He had high hopes, a strong and tender heart, and wisdom born of figuring out way too much on his own. He tells me now that he was immediately drawn to me. I was to him as well, but not in the same way. I had a feeling that our lives would somehow be connected, I just didn't know how. So when Fredelin had the opportunity to come to the States for schooling, we invited him to come to Austin. He would be able to intern at our church as he gained his education. It seemed like a perfect fit.

In the first year of Fredelin's time in Austin, our friendship blossomed. He was an incredible listener, and his faith was strong. He consistently and faithfully pointed me to Jesus. His sense of humor kept me laughing. Something deep and beautiful was building, something beyond ourselves, something gloriously redemptive.

Three years after meeting, when I walked down the aisle into Fredelin's arms as his bride, the full circle picture was evident to all. There wasn't a dry eye in the place as we reflected on it all during the reception: We lost Caleb. Out of his loss, my parents built the Caleb House. Fredelin came to the Caleb House with his own share of losses. He and I fell in love and ultimately married. My parents gained a son through the loss of another son. Fredelin gained a family after the loss of his own.

Fredelin and I have now been married for 4 years. We have a little boy named after Caleb. My brother's name was Caleb Sterling. Our boy's name is Sterling Fredelin.

Full circle.

Redemption.

Joy.

Though I Walk Through the Valley

Kim Taylor Henry

Yea, though I walk through the valley of the shadow of death, I will fear no evil; for thou art with me; thy rod and thy staff they comfort me.
—PSALM 23:4 (KJV)

Though my father believed in God and regularly attended a local church, for most of his life he thought Jesus had only been a great man. But his personal savior? No. My mother, sister and I prayed for his salvation, but he remained stubborn, insisting he needed "proof."

In his eighty-fifth year, Daddy stopped trying to lightly dismiss the importance of belief in Christ. He asked serious and pointed questions and gave thought to our answers. Finally, the miracle happened. He said to us, "Jesus Christ is my Lord and Savior." From that moment on, we noticed a softening in his nature. He expressed his love for my mother in ways he never had before. He showed a new patience and tolerance. His love for others expanded.

For nearly 10 years Daddy had been suffering with emphysema, though he never complained. I lived over 2,000 miles away, but had flown out for brief visits many times in response to calls of concern from my sister, who lived close to our parents. One May, though I did not receive any phone calls to come, I suddenly felt a need to visit my father. When I arrived, I realized, with a sinking heart, why God had nudged me to be there. But little did I know that this would be the first in a series of moments—and amazing serendipities—that would put God's great love and perfect timing on display.

As a parent does not always see their child changing before her eyes, I do not believe my mother or sister had seen what I saw when I arrived. Daddy was different. I felt he was dying. I had planned to stay less than a week, but decided to extend my visit to be with him as he passed. Even a short while before, I would not have been able to do that. But less than 2 months earlier, after 25 years of practicing law, I had stopped working. Now I was free to stay with my parents for as long as they needed me.

Daddy and I sat and talked longer than we had in ages. He told me stories of his childhood. We looked at photos. I gave him a haircut. We spent precious hours together.

When I had been there almost 2 weeks, Daddy had a particularly good day, and my hopes were up. I missed my husband and three children, and so I decided to return home to them. I made my flight reservation, packed my bags, and arranged for transportation to the airport. But I did not feel peace. I prayed, "Please Lord, let me know what I should do. Should I stay, or should I leave?" Within minutes I felt strongly I should stay. I unpacked my bags, canceled my reservations, and cried, long, hard, and deep, because I knew why God was telling me to stay.

I did not know where to turn or how to help Daddy. Again, God intervened to guide the way. As I was driving, I "just happened" to see, in her yard, a neighbor I had not seen in a long time. I stopped to say hello. I told her about my father. She suggested I call hospice. I knew nothing about this particular hospice, but when I called, they came quickly, providing much-needed assistance and support.

My father had always belonged to the local Methodist church. Recently, he had talked of joining the Presbyterian church instead. He wanted to be buried in their cemetery. We called the minister and told him the situation. The next evening, he and three church elders came to my parent's house. After praying together, we all gathered around my father's bedside. For a day he had not spoken, nor opened his eyes. Yet, in the presence of our little group, he struggled to briefly open one eye, and uttered what turned out to be his final words: "Am I a Presbyterian yet?" The ministered confirmed that indeed he was. I could feel God smiling.

Less than 48 hours later, God led my father home. But before He did, He paused—for me and for my father.

It was a Sunday afternoon. I had left with my niece on a difficult task, but one that we felt was important—to purchase a handsome shirt for my father to wear for his triumphant journey home. While at the store, we got a phone call. My father had passed on. With tears of grief flowing, we ran to the car and drove to my parent's house. I was so upset with myself for not having been with him when he left this earth. My sister was on their front porch. "He's waiting for you!" she cried. He had stopped breathing, but his heart was still beating. I ran into his room and said my final goodbye. Within seconds of when I stopped talking, his heart stopped.

That's when we noticed the first of many little "coincidences" that we knew were signs from God. We looked at the bag holding the shirt we had bought for Daddy. In bold letters it read, "Lord and Taylor." My father's last name was Taylor!

We dreaded picking out a cemetery plot. Not only was it painful, but my mother had never been decisive. We envisioned hours of debate. Yet, when we arrived, my mother, who had not been in that cemetery before, pointed quickly

I unpacked my bags, canceled my reservations, and cried, long, hard, and deep, because I knew why God was telling me to stay.

to one area on the map. When we went to it, she walked to a spot and announced that was the place. We suggested a few alternatives, but she stood firm. We purchased the first plot for Daddy, then added a second next to it, which would one day be for my mother. The two plot numbers were 689 A and B. When I made reservations for my family to come to the service, my mother asked me for the flight number. I shook my head in wonder as I read it to her. "It's Flight 1689."

When my parents first met, my mother had been quite impressed with my father's car. She had even remembered its license plate number, 6363, and had a license plate with the same numbers made as his gift for their fiftieth wedding anniversary. After Daddy died, it hit me. "How many years were you married?" I asked with a smile. "Why, it was 63 years!" she answered.

Shortly after my father's death, my sister heard music coming from my parents' room. The room was empty, and no one had been in it for hours. Yet, from the radio on the nightstand by Daddy's side of the bed, the singer's words flowed. "How good it is to be with Jesus."

My mother had season tickets for the symphony. The next concert was the night after my father's death. My sister and I encouraged my mother to attend and told her we would go with her. "What's on the program?" I asked. "I don't know," my mother said. "This one was listed as 'To be announced.'" When we got there, we felt God's loving embrace as we listened to the scheduled piece—Verdi's *Requiem*.

My father was buried in the cemetery of the Presbyterian church on a rainy Friday afternoon. As we said our farewell to him to an unaccompanied solo of "The Lord's Prayer," I knew Daddy no longer needed answers to his questions. He had them all.

Heavenly Hope in the Heat of July

Amy Catlin Wozniak

Hope is like a harebell trembling from its birth . . .
Faith is like a lily lifted high and white.
—Christina Rossetti

During our last Easter dinner with my stepson, Ryan, an Easter lily nestled in a regal purple pot at the center of our table. As was our tradition, my husband, Michael, had brought it home to me on Good Friday. The lily was a sight to behold, with elegant, bell-shaped ivory flowers extending gracefully in all directions, their sweet fragrance filling our home with the promise of spring. Across the table, Ryan—a young man with a hearty appetite and a quick wit—savored seconds of my new wild mushroom dish as we all laughed and talked for hours, enjoying each other's company.

A couple of weeks after the holiday, the lily's vibrant flowers began to fade, dropping one by one onto the kitchen island where I had moved it so it could soak up more sunlight. Normally, I would have tossed it out, but for some reason—to this day I can't remember exactly why—I felt compelled to try to give it new life. Following the planting instructions I found online, I carefully removed the plant from the purple-foiled pot, exposing one of the ugliest bulbs I had ever seen. I didn't think anything could grow from that, but after the threat of evening frost had passed, I planted it in the bed on the west side of our farmhouse and forgot about it.

That Easter would turn out to be our final sit-down holiday with Ryan. On a July night in 2014, he didn't return home. We searched desperately for him for two days, not knowing where he was or what had happened to him. And then, on the third day, we found him. He had been killed in a gas can explosion.

His death devastated our family. First, there was the raw, immediate grief, followed by the mixed emotions, and then the uncertainty of navigating what comes next.

As the first signs of spring emerged the year after Ryan's passing, memories of our last Easter together flooded my mind, filling me with a sense of loss and sadness. On Good Friday, Michael brought home an Easter lily similar to the one we had the year before. Its beauty offered a pinprick of hope in a world that now felt so dark and uncertain, helping to usher in the season of promise and possibility.

One sunshine-filled May morning in 2015, as I was out walking with my Great Pyrenees, Scarlett, I spotted a small plant that had burst through the soil. Though I had forgotten about it, the distinctive pointed, dark-green leaves gave it away—it was that lily I'd planted after our last Easter with Ryan before his death. My heart skipped a beat as I walked over for a closer inspection. It was still small—but it was early yet.

Intrigued, I began to research more about Easter lilies. I read that these lilies were so named because their beautiful white flowers are used to adorn church altars every year at Easter. One article called Easter lilies "white-robed apostles of hope" because they remind us of the rising of Christ. Even the shape of the flowers is said to represent the tomb's opening.

I also discovered that they typically lay dormant underground for several years before flowering and that—when not cultivated in a greenhouse so they would be ready for Easter—they usually bloom in June, just before the onset of

---

I took solace in tending to the lily, watering it and pulling weeds from around its base. In my heart, I hoped that the flowers would open and bring me a sign.

---

summer. And yet here was this one, defying all expectations by sprouting after just one year. In early June, when the plant began to bud, I couldn't help but feel a sense of wonder and awe. I wondered if those buds would open.

June slipped by, and the small buds remained tightly closed. Disappointment began to settle in on me. Still, I refused to give up. Something inside me urged me to be patient, pray, and trust that the miracle would unfold in its own time.

As the first anniversary of Ryan's death approached, I couldn't help but feel a heavy weight on my heart. The circumstances of his death—a faulty gas can, high temperatures, a spark, and fumes that ignited into a flashpoint—felt so random and wrong. Ryan was only twenty-five. His talent as an artist was just starting to flourish, and I knew his unique drawing style would have taken him far. The thought of all the dreams and possibilities that were shattered in an instant when his life was cut short was almost unbearable.

I took solace in tending to the lily, watering it and pulling weeds from around its base. In my heart, I hoped that the flowers would open and bring me a sign that Ryan's life didn't end with his death—that God was still at work here.

And then, on July 9—the first anniversary of Ryan's passing—I walked outside and saw that the buds that had been tightly closed for so long had finally opened, right on schedule and in God's time, in a beautiful realization of the hope I had planted there. I couldn't help but feel overwhelmed with emotion. During my time of deep mourning, my fragile faith took root, just as the roots of that lily bulb did. I know in my heart the timing of the opening of that "white-robed apostle of hope" was a gift from God.

From that moment on, I began to refer to it as Ryan's Lily. Each year since I planted it, the flower has bloomed during the week of his passing, a bittersweet reminder of the life of a young man taken too soon.

Losing Ryan has challenged our family in ways we could have never imagined, forcing us to confront the fragility of life and the pain of loss. But through it all, we have clung to our faith and to each other, striving to live in a way that reflects the beauty Ry brought to our lives while taking comfort in the knowledge that we will one day be reunited with him. We have found ways to flourish in the face of adversity, just like that Easter lily.

Ryan's Lily, once a centerpiece at our last holiday meal with Ryan, has become a beacon for our family, reminding us that hope can blossom even in the depths of grief. Each year, as that sad anniversary date draws near in the summer, I walk out and see its pure white, trumpet-shaped flower stretched gracefully toward the sun, and I know it's a message of heavenly hope in the heat of July.

God's Mysterious Ways: In the Midst of Mourning

Grief can feel lonely, even in a crowd. It can seem as if nobody understands, as if everyone else is living in a parallel world where everything is normal, a world very close to ours, but not actually touching. But even if you do feel alone—if you have in the past or maybe if you do right now—God sees, and God is there for you.

Maybe you haven't suffered a major loss recently, but even smaller losses can occupy a lot of space in our hearts. Here are some ways to be more aware of God's presence:

- **Pray.** No feeling is too small—or too big—to take to God. If there's something you're missing, the loss of something you're mourning, don't hesitate to pray about it.

- **Seek.** Be aware of how the sense of loss feels in your body—how it's held in your muscles—and how that feeling changes when you sense God's presence.

- **Act.** If you're feeling a sense of loss strongly at a particular time, try to take a moment to stop and ask God to let you feel His presence.

- **Reflect.** In past times of loss, did you feel God with you? How did those times affect your journey toward healing?

O Christmas Tree

Ronald F. Lazenby

And my God will meet all your needs according to the riches of his glory in Christ Jesus.

— Philippians 4:19 (NIV)

As director of the clothes closet for my local church, I had no appointments scheduled for the week before Christmas unless someone was in dire need—and this family certainly was. A mother and her three preteen children were referred to us by a local social services agency. The family was moving into a safe home after living in an abused women's shelter for several months. For the safety of her and her children, the mother had to leave everything at her old home and was starting anew with only the clothing and household items provided by the shelter.

She arrived alone and was a bit timid at first. I imagine she was nervous about being assisted by a man after being in an abusive relationship, but as we "shopped," she soon felt comfortable with me. After finding their sizes on the clothes closet racks, we supplied her with shoes, coats, and seven complete outfits for her and each child. From our stores of donated household goods, we were able to give her cookware and cooking utensils, dishes, glasses, silverware, bath towels, sheets and blankets, bedspreads, pillows, and any other needed household items we had available.

Tears began rolling down her cheeks as we carried the clothing and household items to her car. "I am so grateful for what you have given me, and I hate to ask for more. But do you by any chance have a Christmas tree you could give us? My children do not have one, and I can't afford to buy one."

I shook my head. "I'm sorry, but we don't have one, and it's very unlikely that we'll get one in. But if we do, I'll call you." A Christmas tree had never been donated in the 5 years I had served at the clothes closet. *And why would anyone be getting rid of a Christmas tree the week before Christmas? Maybe the week after, but not now.* Of course, I didn't say that out loud.

We crammed the trunk of her car as full as possible and then stacked the bags of clothing in the front and back seats so high she could not see out of her rearview mirror. Her car was so full that even if we had a tree for her, it wouldn't have fit.

She hugged and thanked me again, and she let me know that she still had hope—or maybe she had faith—God would provide one. "Please call me. You have my number if a tree does come in."

I nodded and waved goodbye as she got into her car and drove away.

Within an hour of her departure, another lady entered the clothes closet and asked me if I could help unload her donation. When I got to her car, I could not believe what I saw. She was donating a Christmas tree along with several boxes of ornaments, including some garland and a string of lights. Her family was being relocated to another state and had to be out of their house before Christmas since they were visiting family for the holidays. She did not want to take the decorations with them to their new location.

I immediately called the client while standing by the donor's car. "You are not going to believe this, but we have someone here donating a Christmas tree and decorations. Would you like them?"

Her voice was shaky as she answered. "Oh, yes! I just finished unloading what was given to me and I will be right there."

When I told the donor about the lady's situation and how we had never received Christmas decorations, she was happy a needy family was receiving them and could use them for the upcoming holiday. She even waited to help put the decorations into the client's car, and after loading the car, the three of us had a tearful exchange of hugs.

It could only have been God's intervention to have the tree and all that goes along with it donated the week of Christmas, within minutes of having a request from a needy family. Not only were the client and her family blessed with the needed items, but they, the donor, and I were all blessed to witness God's perfect timing in action.

The week after Christmas, we received handwritten thank-you notes from the mother and each child praising God for leading the donor to us and for our generosity in making it the best Christmas her children had experienced. They were able to open Christmas presents from under their own tree in their newly acquired, peaceful, safe home.

All of My Ways

Betty Meissner

Trust in the Lord *with all your heart and do not lean on your own understanding. In all your ways acknowledge Him, and He will make your paths straight.*

—Proverbs 3:5–6 (NASB)

Waiting for the green light at the intersection with my foot on the brake, I used the moment to look at the map of Green Bay, Wisconsin. The next thing I knew, my car bumped into the one in front of me. I glanced up to see the driver jump out of his car and stride back to mine with an angry look. "I'm so sorry. I was looking down at the map," I explained. When he saw the map spread out before me, he replied, "Oh, you just rolled into me." Mollified, he got back in his car as the light changed.

Shaken and thanking God for taking care of that uncomfortable moment, I continued up the street. Earlier, I had dropped my husband, George, off at the company where he would be interviewing most of the day for an electrical engineering position. He suggested that I look for a place to live, just in case he got the job.

Not feeling comfortable driving in a strange city and not knowing where to start, I asked God to help me. The image of a row of duplexes popped into my mind. The previous evening George—who had lived in this area with his first wife and children before they moved to the West Coast—had given me a tour of his old neighborhood. Just two blocks from the house where they used to live was a street with more duplexes than I had ever seen.

If I could find something close to the kids' old neighborhood, they would have instant friends! Fifteen-year-old Heidi and twelve-year-old Troy had been through a traumatic year with their parents' divorce, moving to California for a year, and now moving back again.

I could relate. I left my home state of Illinois with a divorce pending to live near my daughter in eastern Colorado, and then, a year later, moved to a different part of Colorado to attend a university in Greeley. That move had been the beginning of a series of fortuitous events that led me to a happiness I couldn't have imagined.

Two years earlier, I had been on a very different housing search. I had just quit my job and staked all my assets on finishing my teaching degree, and had arrived in Greeley with no place to live. The thin-walled student housing at the university vibrated with headache-inducing loud music, and a dark, dank off-campus basement space had given me nightmares. I prayed, "God, I leave the finding of a place to live in your hands." Falling into a restful sleep, I didn't wake until morning.

As I went to McDonald's for breakfast, I was filled with peace. When I came back, I found the answer to my prayer in the form of a handwritten note on the bulletin board at the Student Union that listed an apartment for a reasonable rent with phone number. After assuring the lady with a heavy German accent that I would not be having loud parties overhead, I was given the address of a house 11 blocks off campus. When I drove under the tall, arching trees on the shady street to a white brick house with black shutters and a swing on the front porch, I couldn't believe it! After barely glancing at the three small rooms upstairs, and a lengthy interview by the landlords, I was accepted to be their tenant.

Ruth and Rudy enfolded me into their lives. The first year I lived there I spent hours listening to their stories of life in Germany and immigrating to the States with their children. When they told me that their oldest son, George, was in the process of divorce, I felt a kinship with him. My own children were adults and on their own, but his were still living at home.

The following summer, George sent his children alone to visit their grandparents in Greeley. Ruth was nervous about keeping them entertained and asked if I would help. "We're having ice cream with fresh raspberries. Come join us!" As I entered the kitchen and saw Heidi and Troy standing there with expectant looks on their faces, I felt an instant rapport! In between my summer classes we went to movies, played card games, and on the Fourth of July sat on a blanket watching the parade.

Two weeks after they left, George came by himself to Greeley for a family reunion. Ruth had asked me to come down and join them in the backyard. I had seen George standing in the driveway the day before from upstairs window and recognized him from the family photo album Ruth had shown me.

About three in the afternoon, I made my way down to the backyard. Rudy walked me over to George and introduced us. Shortly into the conversation, we realized we were kindred spirits. Moving to the swing on the front porch, George asked about my experience of divorce. We both had been committed to our marriages, but our spouses wanted out. We shared a strong faith in God, reading the Bible daily and attending church regularly. Two hours later, George's sister came look-

I prayed, "God, I leave the finding of a place to live in your hands."

ing for him and chided us for ignoring the rest of the family. Joining them in a large circle on the patio, we sat next to each other chatting till midnight.

The next morning, Ruth telephoned me. "Would you please bring down those chickens I stored in your fridge?" When I entered the kitchen, she invited me to join them for breakfast. As it was Sunday morning, George asked. "May I accompany you to church?"

When we stood to sing from the same hymnal, our arms bumped. I felt a zing of electricity shoot through me. *Really, Lord?* After Sunday dinner, it was time for Rudy to drive George to the Denver airport. As I gave George a goodbye hug, I murmured, "Maybe we could correspond?" Privately, I thought, *He's probably not a letter writer.*

But on the plane flying back to California, he penned a letter. For the next 11 months, we corresponded daily. Phone calls, cassette tape recordings sharing life histories, and trading visits every other month nurtured our relationship. After my coursework was finished in June, we got married in my church in Greeley with both our families in attendance. The final requirement of student teaching could be arranged wherever I lived.

All during our long-distance courtship, George sought employment elsewhere with the help of a business headhunter. When a former boss in Green Bay recognized George's name on a résumé sent to him, he called to set up an interview for the week after our wedding. He invited George to bring me along.

Cresting the hill of the street with all those duplexes, I saw a lady pounding a "for rent" sign on the lawn. I pulled into the driveway. After a tour of the three-bedroom townhouse, I told her we would take it if my husband got the job.

He did. Within three weeks, we packed up George's household in California and mine in Greeley, and the whole family moved to Green Bay. No sooner had the van pulled out of the driveway than Heidi and Troy made a beeline through the yards to their old neighborhood. The rest of the summer they hung out there. As for me, I was thanking God for the time to adjust to married life with two teenagers again before I got busy with practice teaching in September.

George recalled a church of our denomination within walking distance. After visiting, we joined, and the kids made new friends in the youth group.

With a 6-month lease on the duplex, we started looking for a house to buy in the same school district. Finding two but unable to decide between them, we went round and round. A thought popped into my mind, the same kind of thought that had led me to the duplexes: *If you don't know what to do, do nothing.*

Three weeks later, Heidi came bursting through the deck door exclaiming, "Our house is for sale! Our house is for sale!" The present owners of George's former home in the old

---

Three weeks later, Heidi came bursting through the deck door exclaiming, "Our house is for sale! Our house is for sale!"

---

neighborhood were thinking of selling. They had not even put it on the market yet.

George said that it was up to me as he already knew the house very well. It had everything on my wish list! George pointed out the family room, large cedar closet, and work bench he had added to basement himself. Heidi and Troy showed me their old bedrooms.

Strolling back to the duplex, I asked myself, "How do I feel about moving into the house where George lived with his first wife?" No warning red flags came from above—just grace and peace descended, the same peace that I had felt when God originally led me to the beautiful German couple who would become my parents-in-law. Heidi and Troy turned around and walked backwards facing us. Smiling at them, I nodded my approval. They took off running to tell the neighbors.

With the rest of my assets and George's savings, there was enough for a down payment. Packing up once again, we moved two blocks over. And stayed through high school, college years, and the weddings of Heidi and Troy in our church—where they first met their spouses in the youth group down the road. Through seemingly chance meetings and nudges from above, God guided all of us to exactly where we needed to be.

"Who Cooks for You?"

Louis Lotz

*And remember, I am with you always,
to the end of the age.*
—Matthew 28:20 (NRSVUE)

It was winter, cold and dark, and I was alone. My wife was off visiting family, two weeks of sunning and swimming and playing with our grandchildren.

"You're sure you don't mind if I go?" she'd said. "I feel guilty, me going and you having to stay here and work."

"Of course I don't mind," I replied, truthfully. "It will do you good to see the grandkids, soak up some sun. I'll be fine. Go!"

She went.

I said I'd be fine, and I was. At first. But a week later I was rattling around the house, feeling sad and alone. In all the world my wife is just one person, but that one person is all the world to me. I missed her. Sometimes it is good to be alone, just to make sure you still can be. But I was lonely.

Late one afternoon I decided to take a walk in my woods. I have a theory that walking in the woods draws me closer to God. There is no one else to talk to out there. I slipped into my muck boots, put on my old winter coat, pulled my stocking cap down over my ears, and stepped out into the cold. The sky was a sheet of tin, with occasional dumplings of white cloud. I walked through the snow with the plodding slowness of a barge. It was the violet hour, not quite daylight and not quite dark, and the fading sunlight lay in strips between the trees.

I stopped, as I always do on these excursions, at the big maple where I hung my owl house. It is a barred owl house. A nocturnal predator with large, dark eyes and a 40-inch wingspan, the barred owl sails silently through the darkness on soft feathers with serrated edges that completely muffle sound. The poor field mouse never hears him coming. The owl has a distinctive, eight-note hooting call often phrased as "Who cooks for you? Who cooks for you-all?"

I've always been fascinated by owls, and barred owls in particular. Early one evening, years ago, I saw a barred owl streak down from the sky and smash into the tall grass in the field behind my home. Seconds later he was airborne again, huge wings flapping, his talons clutching a large, writhing snake. It was like a scene from a National Geographic special. When I told my wife, who does not like snakes, what I'd witnessed, she said, "Maybe you could build an owl house and the owl would stay here permanently."

I built the owl house, faithfully following the specifications in a magazine, hung it in the maple at the prescribed height, and then sat back and waited for the owls to arrive. And waited. And waited. It had been 3 years, and still no owls. "Barred owls often nest in tree cavities," said the magazine, "but they will readily nest in a homemade nest box, so long as the box is well situated." Which, apparently, mine isn't. The box has provided lodging, over the years, to squirrels, starlings, and one villainous, hissing possum, but no barred owls. I long ago resigned myself to the fact that I will never hear that eerie, baritone call, "Who cooks for you? Who cooks for you-all?"

That night our house felt especially cold and empty, and I noted, once again, how large a bed can be when you are the only one in it. I read for a while, then put my book aside and clicked off the bedside lamp. Lying half-asleep in the darkness and feeling acutely alone, I heard a haunting, eerie sound coming across the frosty silence of night. At first I thought I had dreamed it, but then it came again: "Who cooks for you? Who cooks for you-all?" I could picture him out there, fluffing his feathers against the cold, calling for his mate. I imagined him inspecting my nesting box and saying to himself, *Yes, this will do quite nicely.* And suddenly, at that exact moment when I'd felt most alone, I realized what I should have known all along—I am never alone. God is always there, always with me.

The Almighty makes Himself known to us through His creation. The owl who calls to you at night. The wren who sings you awake in the morning. The autumn hillside ablaze in color. In so many ways the Father displays His presence, reminding us that we are not alone. The hymn-writer Maltbie Babcock said it best: "This is my Father's world; He shines in all that's fair. In the rustling grass I hear Him pass; He speaks to me everywhere."

Early the following morning, my wife called. She was having a good time, and the grandchildren all said hello.

"And how are you doing?" she asked. "You're getting along OK?"

"I miss you," I said. "But I'm fine."

And I was.

A Job Out of the Blue

Raylene Nickel

*I will make a way in the wilderness and
rivers in the desert.*

—Isaiah 43:19 (RSV)

"Father, please be with John this morning," I prayed. "Grant the lender wisdom. If this farm is right for us, please open the doors to the loan we need to buy it."

I prayed while walking briskly down the driveway of our small country place, willing strength to my prayer. My husband, John, was that very morning in town, sitting in a lender's office presenting a financial package explaining how we would pay for the larger farm we'd looked at only days before and hoped to buy.

It seemed the perfect place, of a size that would let us grow our dreams. A comfortable but modest home. A spacious barn. Pastures for cattle. Lovely trees in the yard and across the farm.

I was back from my walk, sitting in a lawn chair when John returned, crestfallen. "They turned us down," he said, sinking into a chair beside me. "The asking price is too high. We can't make the down payment, and we can't afford the annual payments."

This wasn't the first time we'd looked at a farm, then applied for a loan, only to be turned down. Each time John went to town to visit a lender, I took to the driveway, power walking, storming heaven with my prayers. I'd even written out my prayer and stuck the card in my Power Box, along with other prayers.

Each rejection dashed our hope. Today was no different, and we sat in our lawn chairs in silence. I glanced at John. With a furrowed brow and glistening eyes, he gazed across the yard to the corrals just beyond our small mobile home.

John had built this small farm in Manitoba from scratch. We had a few cattle, horses, and sheep. But the place was too small to support a cow herd of the size needed for John to quit his job on a nearby ranch and support himself by raising cattle full time.

My dreams paralleled his. I loved cattle. I'd grown up caring for livestock on a farm in North Dakota, where my aging mother still kept cows. After college, I moved to Manitoba to work on a ranch, which is where I met John. But after 5 years, my earlier dream of freelance writing kicked in, and I quit my job. After marrying John, I shared his dream of owning a larger place.

Despite rejection from lenders, I kept on praying: "Dear Lord, please find us a place that has open pastures, some of it suitable for haying and grazing; some of it heavily treed. A comfortable-feeling house and yard, and some workable livestock facilities. But in the end, we're willing to go—or stay—where You lead us. Help us to listen."

It wasn't long before John found yet another farm to look at. We set off filled with hope. This farm was more affordable. A rustic log stable hid in the trees, and spreading elms surrounded the old, sagging farmhouse. Overgrown pastures promised grazing for cattle. We believed we could make a home there.

A few days later, John again visited the lender, proposing the purchase of a lower-priced farm. But the lender's response was the same: "I'm sorry, but we can't approve this loan," he said.

The doors to our dreams seemed shut for good. We both focused on our daily chores. It was 1989, and I wrote articles on a typewriter from my office in a town nearby. My work was unpredictable. I never knew from one article to the next where another assignment might come from. My income was erratic, to say the least.

After marrying John, I shared his dream of owning a larger place.

Thoughts of a new farm faded until a weekend visit to my mother in North Dakota. "Have you found a farm yet?" she asked.

"No," I said. "It doesn't look like we'll be able to buy a farm right now."

"What's wrong with this farm?" she asked.

Her question floored me. I hadn't thought she was ready to turn over the reins to her own farm.

Upon returning home, I told John about the opportunity. He responded with silence and a guarded look on his face. It would be a major move for him, leaving the country of his birth and all of the cultural and agricultural norms familiar to him.

Over the coming weeks, I kept silent. We talked more with my mother, but I left the final decision to John.

One day, after he had finished his lunch and was about to step out the door to return to work, he turned to me and asked, "Do you want to go to North Dakota?"

Surprised, I put the question back on him: "Is that what you really want to do?"

He pointed at me and said, "As long as you keep the typewriter going!"

That triggered a flurry of activity to prepare for the move. The first thing we had to do was apply for John's immigration into the United States. The neighboring ranch had sponsored me when I applied for immigration into Canada. Now, as a U.S. citizen, I needed to sponsor John's immigration to my home country.

But when the package of paperwork arrived in the mail, I spread out the papers on my desk and found to my dismay a worrying requirement. As John's sponsor, I needed to prove means of financial stability. As a fledgling freelance writer, my income was anything but stable. To boot, except for one magazine in North Dakota, most of my income came from Canadian outlets, which I would lose when I left.

Suddenly, the weight of our future fell squarely on my shoulders, and I didn't know what to do. As the days unfolded, I said nothing to John as I tried desperately to figure out how to navigate the demands of the paperwork. Even my prayers stalled. I hardly knew how to pray. What I really needed was a job in North Dakota with a steady income, but I didn't know where to begin looking.

One day in my office, I again spread out the application on my desk. I reread the requirements for financial information.

I still had no idea how to fill out that section of the form. Overcome with despair and helplessness, I dropped my head on my desk, sobbing. "Father" was the only word I could pray.

The ringing of my office phone shattered the silence, and I answered it. "Hello, Raylene," said a man's voice. I recognized it as the voice of the editor of the North Dakota magazine I wrote for periodically. "I'm calling to see whether or not you might be interested in a position that just opened up on our magazine staff."

"I'm calling to see whether or not you might be interested in a position that just opened up on our magazine staff."

I was stunned, listening eagerly to his description of the job's details. Of course I accepted on the spot, even though the job was nearly a hundred miles from my mother's farm. From that day, John and I were seemingly catapulted into a river carrying us to our new farm in North Dakota.

Yet it was a river brimming with its own turbulence. John and I were at first separated for several months between the time my work started and his immigration was approved. After a while, I quit my job to be with John on the farm, and as the years unfolded, we worked side by side to build a home from our new cattle farm while I continued freelance writing.

There were plenty of challenges. Through it all I often retreated to a place on the farm I call my Prayer Hill, and there I poured out my heart to God, praying to find His way through the difficulties, which eventually included the death of my dear John.

More than 30 years have passed since we came to this farm, where I still live, write, and care for cattle. The other day, while walking along a fence, I passed a tree-lined wetland John and I called the Lunch Tree Slough. That first year on this farm we often sat in the shade of a soaring cottonwood at lunch time, discussing our work.

On my walk the other day, I stopped to gaze at the beauty of the Lunch Tree Slough. As he had at numerous other places around the farm, John had nurtured volunteer tree seedlings wherever they chose to grow. The seedlings had now become trees, alive with the chorus of robins. John and God had together created the farm of his dreams. As John said only months before his death, echoing my sentiments precisely, "I love our place; I love what we do here."

So many years ago, God guided us right where He wanted us to go, fulfilling our purpose in the process. He closed the doors that were not right and swung wide the one door meant for us when He gave me a job out of the blue.

The Forgotten Skillet and the Iron

Lynne Hartke

*In peace I will lie down and sleep, for you alone,
Lord, make me dwell in safety.*
—Psalm 4:8 (NIV)

What woke me up?
I shifted from my blanketed cocoon in our comfortable bed, being careful not to jostle my sleeping husband, Kevin. I could hear the soft breathing of our dog, Mollie, on the floor—sound asleep. With sensitive canine ears, she would have barked a warning if anything unusual had happened inside or outside the house.

The red numbers on the alarm clock glowed on the nightstand. 1:58 a.m.

Why am I awake? I accessed the possibilities as I willed my groggy brain to focus. *Bad dream? No. Bathroom? Nope.*

I was reluctant to leave my warm bed, but I decided I better investigate. I grabbed my glasses and shuffled down the dark hallway. The soft glow from the streetlights shone through the slits of the blinds on the front window. No beam of light appeared under the bedroom of our grown daughter, Katelyn, who lived with us. She had still been up cleaning the kitchen when I went to bed.

An excellent cook, Katelyn had recently purchased a cast iron skillet to concoct new recipes. Crispy fried chicken, deep-dish pizza, and chocolate-chip skillet cookies were a few of the recent delicious offerings. For last night's meal she had created cheesy-herbed-stuffed chicken wrapped in prosciutto. We devoured every bite.

"Would you like me to wash the skillet?" I had asked as I loaded the dishwasher with plates and utensils.

"Don't touch the skillet!" Katelyn had admonished. "I will do it later." She detailed the cleaning process, involving multiple steps with hot water, coarse salt, and hand drying. "After that, I will heat it on the stove to remove all traces of moisture and then I will oil the skillet to seal it to prevent rusting."

"I will leave it to you," I'd said. Although I was more casual in my kitchen style, having a foodie in the house had taught me to respect the proper care of knives, cookware, and other kitchen gadgets.

Now, still puzzled as to why I was awake, I entered the dark kitchen. Bright red lights beamed from the stove panel. The front right burner was on. Not only that, in the darkness I could see a black shape on the hot surface.

What is that? I wondered, flipping on the overhead light to reveal the cast iron skillet, forgotten on the stove top. The sides and handle were too hot to touch as I quickly turned off the stove and searched for hot pads to move the skillet to the counter.

Wide-eyed and adrenaline surging, I returned to bed, but not to sleep. I rehearsed worse-case scenarios as I planned the conversation I would have with our daughter in the morning.

The entire kitchen could have gone up in flames! We could have all died in our beds! Who forgets to turn off a hot appliance?

The last question had barely formed in my brain when I remembered a family story about my grandmother and another forgotten appliance.

Grandmother Ruth always insisted that my dad and his six siblings be clean and tidy on Sunday mornings when they attended the church near their dairy farm in northern Wisconsin. In the days before polyester, that meant cotton shirts and dresses had to be pressed with a hot iron to remove offending wrinkles. For added crispness, the fabric was lightly sprayed with starch before the final pressing.

The smell of smoldering wood met the family when they returned several hours later. The hot iron had burned completely through the wooden ironing board.

"We need to leave in a few minutes," Grandma yelled up the rickety staircase to the bedrooms on the second level, "or we will be late."

"We're only on time once a year when the clocks change," Grandma muttered to the youngest, Roger, as she gathered dirty dishes from the table and set them in the sink for later.

"Lois, your dress is on the ironing board," she reminded one of the older girls before hurrying to tidy her hair and grab her purse.

In the mad scramble to get the large family out the door, Grandma forgot to unplug the iron. Not only did she forget to unplug it, but she also left the iron face down on the old-fashioned ironing board.

The smell of smoldering wood met the family when they returned several hours later. The hot iron had burned completely through the wooden ironing board. In addition, the iron had melted through the linoleum and continued burning the hardwood floorboards below. A charred triangular imprint remained.

"It was the weight of the iron that saved us," Uncle Roger said when he told me the story. "As the iron fell from the ironing board, the weight pulled the plug from the wall. It was still hot enough to burn the floor, but it did not continue heating and burn down the entire farmhouse."

Did an unseen hand mysteriously pull the plug from the wall? Did that same hand jostle me awake from a sound sleep decades later? I think so.

The details remain uncertain, but what is certain was God's care for us. Two appliances were forgotten by two different women in two separate times in history as they tended to the needs of a family, but God the Father, did not forget. He stepped in and saved both—and those they loved—from certain tragedy. My anger shifted to gratitude as I thanked God for His diligent love and care.

Katelyn was aghast the next morning when I told her of my nighttime adventures. "I could have burned down the house!" she exclaimed.

"God was watching over us," I said, extending grace. "He did it in the past too. Did I ever tell you the story about my grandmother and a forgotten iron?"

God's Mysterious Ways: The Little Things

Sometimes signs of God's presence in our life are so subtle that they're easy to miss. We might wonder, as one of our story authors did, why God would allow us to pursue the wrong relationship, or why we're waking up in the middle of the night for no clear reason. Like road signs, sometimes you have to travel for a while before you see what those little pointers were leading you to.

- **Pray.** Is there something happening in your life that doesn't seem to have a clear purpose? Or would you like to understand better where God is pointing you? Bring it up during your prayer time and open yourself for the response.

- **Seek.** The next time you find yourself getting frustrated over a strange roadblock, instead stop and ask yourself: Where might God be pointing me right now?

- **Act.** Do you think you see where God is pointing you? Embrace it and move forward confidently.

- **Reflect.** Think about major changes in your life from times past. Did God leave any "pointers" for you that you might have missed?

She Casually Stepped Out of the Crowd

Grace Assante

Show me the way I should go, for to you I entrust my life.
—Psalm 143:8 (NIV)

Suffocating air, steaming hot concrete, and cantankerous commuters all competing for a seat on the subway . . . just another August afternoon in New York City. Until the blackout of 2003.

That Thursday I had ridden the subway from my home in Brooklyn to my doctor's appointment in Manhattan. I suffered from a rare and incurable autoimmune disease called dermatomyositis where my white blood cells kicked into overdrive and attacked my muscles. The visit had been full of blessings—my "dermato" was in remission, and the doctor wrote me a prescription for the shingles that festered on my back. The psychological reassurance that this specialist had researched and written articles about my disease was worth his expensive bills and my 90-minute commute both ways.

The first leg of my journey home was uneventful, and the refreshing coolness of the air-conditioned subway car relieved my burning, rashy skin. I changed lines in Lower Manhattan and trudged to the next platform one level down, gulping in the stifling, stagnant air. As the train arrived and the double doors opened, I raced at turtle speed toward an open seat. A young man snagged it before me, but when he stared up into my red, puffy face, he rose and moved away.

"Thank you! Thank you!" I nodded toward him as I sat down.

I closed my inflamed eyes. *Thank You, Lord. Thank You*

"It's a blackout!" A man's strained voice rose from the crowd.

---

for that stranger's kindness. Thank You that my dermato is in remission. Thank you for meds for shingles. Tears welled up as I slumped down to rest on the ride home.

A minute passed. Then another. More passengers boarded. Then a jarring voice: "All passengers off the train. This train is out of service."

A collective groan punctuated by profanity in various languages filled the car. No one moved.

In a few moments: "This train is out of service. Everyone must exit."

The human wall sighed and grumbled as it gradually broke apart and moved toward the open doors. I grunted, rose from my seat, and shuffled behind the herd. As I exited the car, the fluorescent lights flickered, then darkened. AC stopped flowing.

Agitation and confusion heightened as all commuters exited the trains on all the platforms.

"What the—!"

"So much for paying taxes!"

"I'm moving to Florida!"

Two police officers approached the swelling crowd. "Exit the station, folks. There are no trains in service at this station."

No trains at all? Weird. Something's going on. I struggled to keep up with the swaying bodies in front of me as we flowed upward via three staircases and eventually flooded outside, into the waning sunlight and the suffocating blanket of hot air.

I stood in the middle of the sidewalk. A sea of confused and frightened faces looked up and around. A man swung his briefcase and marched past with fierce determination, staring straight ahead. A woman bumped my arm as she careened around me. I dodged through the moving mass until I leaned against the glass front of a shoe store, out of the way.

"It's a blackout!" A man's strained voice rose from the crowd.

The terrorist attack on the World Trade Center had occurred 2 years prior, and the horrid sights, sounds, and smells were still fresh, still painful, and still threatening. It seemed this top-of-the heap city was about to go down again.

Then a worse realization slammed into me. Our 16-year-old daughter was somewhere in the city taking ballet class! "Dear Father in heaven, where is she? Uptown? Midtown? Downtown?"

I fumbled in my bag and grabbed my cell. My hands shook as I checked the lighted screen. No service. "Please protect her, Lord! Please help her find her way home!" *There are millions of people in New York City. Where is my one daughter? Is she stuck in an elevator 30 stories up or trapped several stories underground in a stranded subway car? Will she make it back to Brooklyn?* "Father in heaven—help!"

I shook the cell and smacked it against my palm as if whacking it would bring it to life. *I'll call my husband.* He worked in the city. I punched at the numbers. Still no service. I groaned loudly and scanned around me, but the strange faces neither heard nor cared. Which ballet studio was it? What had she told me? Why hadn't I paid more attention when she left the house this morning? I knew I couldn't walk to all the dance studios.

But something or Someone kept me rooted in place . . . told me not *to move.*

A few shoppers exited the shoe store. Hundreds of office personnel poured out of the skyscrapers. In minutes, the growing horde of pedestrians jostled on the sidewalks and spilled into the streets. Taxis, cars, trucks, and buses honked and swerved, but eventually had to stop, blocked by the glut of people taking over the lanes. With traffic lights shut down, anarchy reigned at intersections. No lights. No law. Soon thousands flowed along the sidewalks and streets, a living river of souls.

Was the blackout the first blow in another assault on the city?

My heart raced, and my face swelled and tightened from the rush of stress on mind and body. I glanced around. What should I do? Look for my daughter? Start walking home?

But something or Someone kept me rooted in place . . . told me *not* to move . . . stay calm. Then . . .

"Hi, Mom! What are you doing here?"

I whirled around. Our daughter casually stepped out of the crowd and smiled at me. I couldn't believe my eyes! A friend was with her, another dancer who had taken class as well. We hugged. It was a miracle. Of all the places I could have been in that moment when the blackout struck—in the crowds and chaos of the streets as people poured out of the buildings in confusion—I had arrived at exactly the right place, at exactly the right time, to find my daughter.

"Oh, thank You, Lord! Thank You, Lord! Thank You, Lord!" I looked from one beautiful face to the other.

"What's going on?" our daughter wondered. "We were sitting on the subway, and the conductor told us to get off the train."

I hugged her again and tried to sound calm. "It's a blackout. Don't know why or how, but the city's gone dark."

She shrugged and glanced at her friend. "Guess our dinner plans in Chelsea are off. I'll text the others."

She soon realized that texting was impossible. I waited for her to exhibit some form of fear or panic, but she seemed to take our situation in stride. Perhaps it's because she grew up in New York, where inconvenience and aggravation are part of daily life.

"Guess we'll be walking home tonight, huh, Mom?" Our daughter's bright voice was like the final bell of a professional fight. It was a win. I was already home.

As long shadows fell across the street, she took my arm, and the three of us started walking, one small step at a time. The prospect of trekking 7 miles in a heat wave didn't discourage her or her friend one bit, and the fact that we were together made the journey possible for me. If she hadn't been with me, if she hadn't stepped out of the crowd, I couldn't have made it home. I would have been sitting on a curb somewhere in the dark streets of Manhattan, waiting for my husband to pick me up and carry me home.

At twilight we arrived at the Brooklyn Bridge, where Marty Markowitz, the Brooklyn borough president, stood in the middle of the pedestrian walkway, holding a megaphone. The brilliant orange sunset was behind him. "Welcome back to Brooklyn! How sweet it is! You're almost home!"

The three of us shook our heads and laughed.

A Connection across Oceans

Lynn Spotts Carmichael

*My sheep listen to my voice; I know them,
and they follow me.*

—John 10:27 (NIV)

It was early in the morning, already hot and humid, with thunderstorms forecast for later in the day. I had barely slept. Everything in my life seemed to be closing in on me—new job responsibilities, new marriage, and the memory of traumatic incidents that made me wonder about my faith.

Today my thoughts were all centered on my father. He had been in and out of the hospital several times in the past year with everything from a string of mini-strokes and seizures to a colon cancer diagnosis. I had kidded him that he was like a cat—he had nine lives and always seemed to land on his feet. But this time was different.

The phone call I had always dreaded came in about 4 a.m. It was my mother, frantic and incoherent. All I could make out was, "Come to the hospital quick!" My husband and I jumped out of bed, threw on some clothes and drove silently to the hospital. When I stepped off the elevator, I knew. As

I walked toward my father's room, feeling as if I was moving in slow motion, I could hear sobbing. My father, the spiritual leader of my family, the man who taught me to "hang tough," had died at the age of seventy-one.

The next several hours were surreal. In a dream-like state, I wrote my father's obituary, reflecting on how much he had given to his church and the community around him. I was especially proud that my father, while a lieutenant in the Korean War, had befriended and led a young Korean orderly named Woo Bok Kee to Christianity. After the war, my father supported this man financially and spiritually in building several churches in South Korea over the years. Although the two did not speak or write often, there remained an inseparable bond between them.

I went to my parents' house later that morning and was caught up in the overwhelming flow of family and friends bringing food, hugs, and emotional support. But amid the shock and the shared grief, there was a thought that wouldn't leave me: I was convinced in my *head* that my father was at peace in heaven; however, my *heart* needed confirmation from God.

Even as I thought this, I overheard a long-time neighbor and friend telling someone about a phone call he had received at the house while my family was at the funeral home. My ears perked up. The call had been from South Korea.

"Mack," I said, "would you mind repeating the details of that phone call for me?" It had only been six hours or so since my father's death. I thought, *What could have prompted an overseas call at this time?* Mack excitedly told me that the call had been from a Korean man, Woo Bok Kee. Apparently, in his prayer and devotion with the Lord, the Holy Spirit had told him of my father's passing. He was praying for our entire family in our time of grief.

"Thank You, God!" I prayed under my breath. This astounding event—that a man on the other side of the world had known of my father's passing—showed me that God had been with my father, guiding every detail, as he left this world. Now my heart was, and still is, at peace, for I knew that my father was Home.

The Perfect Road Trip

Amanda Pennock

*The Lord is my strength and my shield;
my heart trusts in him, and he helps me.*
—Psalm 28:7 (NIV)

It was another hot summer day in southeast Texas. The year was 2020, and just a few months earlier a new virus labeled Covid-19 had emerged, causing a lot of hospitalizations and deaths. The entire world had changed. We could not leave the house without wearing masks and were advised not to even go anywhere except to the store and to doctor appointments.

That morning my husband had woken up and was not feeling well. We called a local clinic and set up an appointment for a Covid test. When we arrived, my husband checked in and my brother and I asked if we could also be tested. The next open appointment was the following day, so we returned for our tests then. We were told it would be 5 to 7 days for the results to come back, and that we all were to quarantine until then.

Needless to say, it was a very stressful couple of days. Little did I know that this was just the beginning of a week that I will never forget.

I woke up the next day in a much better state of mind. My husband was feeling better, and it was a beautiful, sunny day. I was relaxing outside in my chair when my phone rang. It was my cousin in Georgia telling me that my uncle had died. The services would be held on Friday—just two days after the call came on Wednesday.

How would I be able to make it in time? Flying was not recommended because of the virus, and it would be a 13-hour drive from Texas. Plus, I just had that Covid test, and the results weren't due back for another 4 to 6 days. I was worried about exposing others, but how could I not go? My uncle had always been there for me. He was the only positive father figure in my life.

When I was young, I got involved in drugs and alcohol, and things got so desperate that I had lost hope. My uncle sat me down and told me about Jesus, explaining that if I accepted Him as my Lord and Savior, I would live in eternity. That message changed my life forever. I wanted to go to the funeral, pay my respects, and tell others what he had meant to me.

As I hung up the phone, my head was spinning. *What do I do?* If I was going to make the service, I would have to pack and head out soon—the next day at the latest. I knew what I had to do.

I went to my bedroom, got on my knees, and asked God for guidance. "God, I really want to go. Please let me know if it's Your will." Prayer finished, I felt much better. *He will let me know.*

The next morning, I woke up and went about my morning routine—coffee, cereal, and checking my email. I could not believe my eyes. There was a message in my inbox from the medical clinic with my Covid test results. Negative. It had only been 48 hours since my test. My result was the only one that had come back; my husband and brother were both still waiting on their results. They would not be able to go, since they didn't know if they were contagious, but God's message was undeniable.

I would go to the funeral, just God and me.

Filled with gratitude and amazement, I started running

I would have to get on the road as soon as possible to have any hope of making it in time. It would take me 2 days to get to Georgia, and it had been a long time since I had driven that far by myself.

---

through the house, throwing clothes into a suitcase. It was already late afternoon when I finished packing, and I would have to get on the road as soon as possible to have any hope of making it in time. It would take me 2 days to get there, and it had been a long time since I had driven that far by myself. Even so, all I could feel was excitement.

I left my house at 6 p.m. Thursday evening. I said a prayer as I backed out of the driveway. "God, please be with me and help me to be able to speak at my uncle's service."

That first night, I only had about 3 hours of sunlight before I had to stop for the night at a small town in Louisiana. I got little sleep, because I had to get up early. I had another

10 hours to drive in order to get to the service, which was scheduled for 3:30 in the afternoon.

I left the hotel in Louisiana next morning while it was still dark out. What a beautiful morning. I could feel God's presence all around me. I could see Him in the sunrise; I could see Him everywhere.

The drive went quickly, and before I knew it, I passed the "Welcome to Georgia" sign. Only a few more miles to the hotel that I had reserved for the night. Should I stop? Would I have time? I wanted to check in, get freshened up, change clothes. By now it was after noon, and I still had over an hour to go. "God, it's in your hands," I told Him.

I stopped at the hotel and the desk clerk told me that my room wasn't ready. Oh well. I would get back on the road and check in after the service. But then, as I was headed for the door, the hotel clerk called me back over and told me she had one room available. It would be an upgrade to a suite for the same price. Would I be interested in taking that room? *Wow, God is so good!*

After I changed, I put the address to the service in my GPS and headed down the highway. As I took the last left into the cemetery, I recognized the place—it was where my dad had been buried.

I pulled into the parking lot. Right behind me, a van bearing the name of the funeral home pulled in. My heart skipped a beat. It couldn't be, could it? "OK, God, now you're just showing off!" I said out loud.

Wow. What an amazing God we serve. After 800 miles and two days of driving, I arrived at the cemetery at exactly the same time as my uncle.

I thought about everything that had to have taken place for this to happen, from my negative Covid test coming back after just 48 hours to the perfect timing of the trip that brought me to the service exactly when I needed to be there. This was definitely too amazing for coincidence.

At the funeral I was able to speak about what a great man my uncle was, how he loved God, how he always tried to bring happiness to others with his corny jokes. I was able to comfort my cousins and give a message of hope in a time of such uncertainty. God let us all know that He is still in control, and that our hope is in Him.

Father's Day

David Stauffer, as told to Kathleen Stauffer

"For my thoughts are not your thoughts, neither are your ways my ways," declares the Lord. *"As the heavens are higher than the earth, so are my ways higher than your ways and my thoughts than your thoughts."*
—Isaiah 55:8–9 (NIV)

I don't recall what the weather was like that day, lying in my room at St. Mary's Hospital in Rochester, Minnesota. I have no idea what I had for breakfast; I don't have a memory now, years later, of being in pain or not. But I knew two things for certain that morning: it was Father's Day, and I would be alone.

My wife, Kathy, was in Texas helping a daughter and her children move from one house to another. The hallways outside my room were mostly quiet. Muffled footsteps in the hallway along with voices from the nurses' station down the hall filtered into the room. Sitting up, I saw the various colored pictures that the grandchildren had taped on the wall the day before, bringing to mind the faces of loved ones who had visited.

The ringing phone interrupted my rambling thoughts. Who would call me on the hospital phone line? Planted among a plastic container of water, Kleenex box, my cell phone, and various educational and spiritual pamphlets, it kept ringing. I answered.

"Hello. Is this David Stauffer?" a man's voice asked.

"Yes," I replied.

"I'm Eugene Stauffer," he stated quietly, "and I would like to visit you."

Drowsy from medications and feeling out of sorts, I thought it perhaps a cruel prank. My own deceased father's name was Eugene Stauffer. However skeptical, I agreed, and wondered if anyone would show up. Minutes later, a man knocked on the half-opened door, walked in, and introduced himself, again, as Eugene Stauffer. He shook my hand and held it a moment or two as we studied each other. Of average height and dressed in black pants, a white cotton shirt, and suspenders, he did not resemble my father at all. He smiled easily, and we visited comfortably about our families and work experience. I learned he was a Mennonite farmer and church leader who lived in Iowa, was a father of eight, and had a herd of a hundred milk cows.

After several minutes, I expressed my surprise and curiosity over his name being the same as my father's. He smiled a bit and shrugged his shoulders, having no explanation to offer. I went on to talk about my dad and how he had worked for Chicago Northwestern Railroad after returning from World War II and had retired after 40-some years. As we talked, I could picture my dad in retirement—enjoying fishing, golfing, refinishing woodwork in their home, and wintering in Arizona with his wife, my mother, Roberta. I also shared with this man, Eugene, about my father's own suffering and that my dad passed in 2003, exactly 10 years before.

I dozed off while we were visiting, so I missed saying goodbye and expressing "thanks for coming" to Eugene Stauffer. Nor did I, with my mind hazy from the medications, think to ask him why he had come to visit in the first place; later I imagined that it was some sort of volunteer service. But the visit was a lasting blessing for me.

Albert Einstein is often credited with saying, "Coincidence is God's way of remaining anonymous." What are the odds that someone with my father's name would come to visit me on Father's Day, bringing me comfort at a time I would otherwise have been alone? There are no random happenings with our sovereign God.

Thanks to prayers from family members, and local churches—both our own and others in the area—my health improved. Because of Eugene Stauffer, my dad, and Eugene Stauffer, my surprise visitor, I had an experience of lovingkindness that I carry with me continually and have remembered every Father's Day since then.

Sean's Text Message

Jinx MacMillan

You turned my wailing into dancing; you removed my sackcloth and clothed me with joy, that my heart may sing your praises and not be silent. LORD, my God, I will praise You forever.

—PSALM 30:11–12 (NIV)

Late one night in our beach house, I sat in our bed by myself quietly reading. My family had just spent the weekend enjoying sun and sand together in Ocean City, New Jersey, and everyone else had left to return to their respective homes. My cell phone suddenly signaled me of an incoming text.

The message said: "I left a package for you at THE FRONT DESK."

I texted back: "Who is this?"

Response: "Sean."

I texted back: "My Sean?"

Response: "Yes, your Sean."

All I could do for a moment was stare at the phone, stunned. How could this be? My Sean—my son—was in heaven.

Sean's death happened just 4 weeks after our last vacation together, a family cruise. He had returned to his studies at Palm Beach Atlantic University in Palm Beach, Florida, preparing for the final exams of his sophomore year in between surfing with his buddies.

He and four other students went out to a Kenny Chesney concert. On the way back, the driver, who was drunk, drove off the road, rolling the car six times before it stopped. Those without seatbelts—including Sean—died. The three surviving students were terribly injured.

This happened just prior to finals week at the school. The college president and the faculty and staff of the university were very caring and attentive to the student body as well as to us, the parents and families of those affected by the crash. We were given rooms in the "presidential suites" at the university to stay in while preparing for the memorial service. It was during that time that I truly realized how much Sean's friends looked up to him because of his love for the Lord. They considered him a brother.

The Family Church of Palm Beach, directly next to the campus on the Intracoastal Waterway, held a celebration of life memorial service with over 900 people in attendance, including students and families. We were overwhelmed by the powerful and spontaneous outpouring of love and brotherhood for our son and the other student who died in the accident, Park. The blessings we received and the friendships we made that day would remain strong for many years to come.

Sean and Park were surfers. Following the service, we four parents and our families were taken to the nearby beach, where we experienced a farewell tradition that I'm told is practiced by surfers worldwide. First, we were embraced in a huge circle of surfers and students. We were each given a lei of fresh plumeria flowers that had been handmade by one of Sean's classmates and fellow surfers. The scent of these flowers is truly heavenly. Over a hundred young men and women

Sean's death happened just four weeks after our last vacation together, a family cruise.

gathered on the beach with us as they sang and prayed. In addition to those in the circle, there were a multitude of others standing and sitting outside the circle in the sand, as a part of the whole. At a given signal, all those surfers picked up their surfboards and ran into the ocean. Two of these carried a pair of surfing shorts, one of each belonging to our sons, which they passed down the line from one surfer to the next as they straddled their boards far out in the water. Then, as a suitable wave approached, each surfer in cadence, it seemed, stood up and rode toward the beach.

The maturity of those students stands out to me as powerfully today as it did then. They comforted us with words and love beyond measure. The following week, several of Sean's close friends joined us at our own church, nearly a thousand miles away from their school in Florida.

Now, a year after Sean's passing, I stared at the text I'd received. The front desk? Memory flooded back.

It was April 1, the last evening of that family ocean cruise with me, my husband, Sean, my sister, her husband, and her two daughters plus a friend. All these cousins were on spring break from college. At 4 a.m., Sean and his cousin Lauren woke us up with a phone call. Posing as a person of authority from the cruise line, Lauren said, "Hello, this is Natalie from *the front desk*. We have your son here. He was caught cheating in the casino and taking other peoples' poker chips. Please come down here to the front desk immediately."

Still barely awake, I had assured her that Sean was more likely to have reported someone else for cheating than he was to have done so himself. I told her I would go down to the front desk. I fumbled around for my clothes in the dark so as not to awaken my husband. Just as I was ready to go, Sean and Lauren burst through the door with a chorus of "April fools!" We all laughed ourselves silly! They sure pulled it off with flair! We talked about it for weeks afterward.

Who else would have known to text me with that specific reference to the "front desk"? I glanced over to identify the phone number of the caller. I could not believe my eyes. The last four digits of the number were 1986, the year of Sean's birth! Of course, I immediately called the number, but all I got was a weird wrong-number noise.

I understood immediately that this was a miracle. God had allowed me to have this special message from Sean to comfort me in a time of grief and confirm our faith in His wonderful plan. It was not the last time He would send me signs of His love and care, but I will always remember this extraordinary moment.

Over the ensuing 17 years God has blessed us with special heartfelt friendships and bonds from Sean's memorial service, forged through tears. Those who were students then, now have families of their own. What a lifetime gift we have received through their thoughtful prayers, photos, texts, letters, emails, and occasional visits.

Ours is a mighty God. Nothing is too small or sublunary for Him to show His extraordinary love and comfort at any time, in any way.

Against the Current

Shirley Gould

*They search the sources of the rivers
and bring hidden things to light.*

—Job 28:11 (NIV)

Enjoying the last days of summer, we slathered our offspring with sunscreen and traveled on a new pontoon boat down the Tennessee River to spend time on our friends' land in southern Tennessee. After we picnicked, we let the kids play in the water. My daughters, ages four, eight, and twelve, loved spending time with our friend Deborah's son, age five, and her daughter, age 14. The oldest girls sunbathed while the younger ones made mudpies at the shallow edge of the river.

My husband and a missionary friend who had joined us for the outing brought a canoe along. The two men decided to paddle upstream and drift back to the pontoon to rejoin our group while Deborah, her husband, and I relaxed with the children.

When the kids began to get weary, we decided to ride in the pontoon boat and fish for a while. As I waded into the water and helped my daughters get on the boat, Deborah's son began slipping through his inner tube.

When his scream for help pierced the air, we jumped into action. Deborah and her husband were too far away to reach him. Being the closest one, I grabbed the boy, who was flailing his arms, afraid that he would sink. He calmed as I helped him to the safety of the pontoon—but I went into full-blown panic mode when the diamond of my engagement ring caught on his life jacket, causing the ring to slip off my finger and disappear in the muddy Tennessee River.

"Nobody move! My ring just went to the bottom of the river." I thought I was going to be sick.

The ring was a cherished treasure. The one-carat diamond surrounded by a leaf pattern with eight smaller diamonds had been placed on my hand when my husband proposed. It was a moment I'll never forget. I looked to see if he was paddling the canoe in our direction, but he was too far away to help with my crisis.

Deborah, her husband, and I searched in a grid-like fashion, feeling the muddy river bottom for the diamond ring. The swift current of the river added to our dilemma while the muddy water made visibility impossible. The tears filling my eyes didn't help me see any more clearly. My angst grew with each passing second. Desperate to find the ring, we dredged the river bottom for 20 minutes, going over and over the same area. When it seemed we weren't going to find it, I stopped everyone who was searching and prayed for a miracle.

After saying amen, I let out a breath I didn't realized I'd been holding. "Let's look for a few more minutes," I told my friends.

"I'm going upriver to look for it." Deborah moved away from our search area.

"But, Deborah, the current is bringing the water in this direction. It won't be up there," I argued. "Searching downriver may be a better—"

Before I finished my sentence, she reached down and picked up my ring. My white gold, diamond-embellished miracle sparkled in the afternoon sun. I was elated, and so very thankful.

How did my ring land upriver? Why did Deborah decide to go against the current to extend our search? Only God could orchestrate the answer to my heartfelt prayer in such a mind-blowing fashion. Only God.

A New 20-Year Friend

D'Ann Mateer

*Therefore, encourage one another and build up
one another, just as you also are doing.*
—1 Thessalonians 5:11 (NASB)

We were empty nesters, our youngest child having left for college a couple of years earlier. And we were a bit restless, even though we couldn't have articulated it as such. We needed a change. An adventure. Something that was just for us after years of life being about our kids. When my husband got an unexpected call to take on a temporary—6 months, max, he said—job in Austin, a city 3 hours from where we'd lived our entire married life, we felt the Lord urging us in that direction.

So we moved. Moved away from family. Moved away from longtime friends. My husband jumped into his new job—a huge, all-consuming job. A job that, after a few months, we realized would last much longer than 6 months. With the knowledge that our city adventure would be extended (we'd originally rented an apartment within walking distance of the vibrant downtown), we decided to purchase a place to live. But not a house. No, we indulged in what had been for us a long-held dream—a few years spent living the city life in a high-rise building, the 360 Residential Condominiums.

Yet this empty-nest adventure in a new city was not everything I had hoped for. I'd been a published author, but suddenly had no new projects on the horizon. I'd made a couple of new friends from church, but the one I'd bonded with most deeply at that point would soon move to California for her husband's job. And moving meant downsizing to one car, because the condo came with only one parking space.

So when the time finally came, I went to the high-rise life dragging my feet a bit. I was lonely. I was bored. I was unmotivated. Not only that, but the condo was bare—our new furniture hadn't yet been delivered, nor had any of our old furniture that had been in storage near our previous house. We were living on lawn chairs with a TV and wi-fi.

One night, I decided to have a look through the member list of the Facebook group for residents on the off chance there might be someone with whom we had a mutual friend. With a less-than-faith-filled prayer that I would find a friend, I scanned the list, seeing nothing.

Until one name caught my eye: Mattie Hildebrand. Beneath her name, something in the vicinity of a hundred mutual friends. Below her, Mike Hildebrand, also with many mutual friends.

My breath caught and I looked over at my husband. "The Hildebrands. Mike and Mattie. Do you remember them? From Tres Dias?"

"I do. Why?"

"They live here. In this building."

"What? Why don't you message—"

"I'm messaging her right now," I said as my fingers flew over the keyboard.

Hi, Mattie. I don't know if you remember me, but we crossed paths for a while in the North Texas Tres Dias community. Jeff and I moved to Austin a couple of years ago and recently bought a condo in the 360. Imagine my surprise as I crossed through the names in the Facebook group and saw you and your husband! Do you still live here? (I assume so.) We'd love to reconnect at some point.

It didn't take long to receive her reply.

Oh my goodness!! I'm so thrilled to see this!!!!!! What unit are you in?? Are you here now? Do you have a church home??? Nope I'm not excited at all!!!!!!!!!!

We set a time to meet for coffee the following week. And that's when the most amazing story unfolded.

When we'd known each other nearly 20 years earlier, we'd been acquaintances with many mutual friends. We'd both worked in a spiritual renewal retreat movement. But not long after our first meeting, I pulled back from my involvement to pursue my dream of being a published author.

And yet she remembered me, even though we'd lost touch all those years ago.

I told her how I came to be in that city, and that building. Then she told me their story. How they had lived in the Middle East for over 10 years while her husband, an engineer, built high-rise buildings, that they had purchased the condo a year and a half earlier. Their college-aged kids had lived in their condo on the sixteenth floor until 6 months earlier, when Mike and Mattie had moved back to the States and their children moved on to apartments of their own.

We both sat dumbstruck. We'd each moved to a new-to-us city and into the same condo building without having seen or heard about each other's lives in many years.

"I've been praying for a friend," she told me.

"So have I," I replied.

The quick depth of that friendship was nothing other than the Lord. Not only did He put us six floors from each other, but He'd given us a bit of long-ago history together so that we weren't starting from scratch.

We both sat dumbstruck. We'd each moved to a new-to-us city and into the same condo building without having seen or heard about each other's lives in many years.

We remained in that condo and city for only two more years. Two years of coffee dates in our condos or coffee shops around us. Two years of dinners together with our husbands. Two years of hanging out at the pool. Two years of angst over grown kids and husbands' jobs and life in general. Two years of bearing one another's burdens, of sharing sorrows and joys. All within a quick elevator ride.

Our friendship became even more important when the Covid pandemic hit. When all the public spaces inside and outside of the condo building shut down. But my friend was, again, just an elevator ride away. And since neither of us had been anywhere or seen anyone, we felt safe. We kept each other sane. We even went for walks up and down the parking garage instead of venturing out into the somewhat deserted city streets.

As much as I was glad to go "home" when my husband's job came to an end, I grieved to leave my new-old friend behind. Those 2 years of friendship felt more like twenty. It was as if all the years in between the time we knew one another before—each of us with kids at home—and later—with all our kids grown—were filled in supernaturally by the Lord. As if we'd been friends all along instead of finding one another so many years later in a 44-story building in a small city.

It was such a bond that, 3 years on, we still talk often, our friendship vibrant and strong. We still support and listen and pray for each other. And we deeply cherish the times we get to see one another in person.

Others might deem our sudden proximity to each other as a coincidence. But we know it was an answered prayer—the answer had begun long before either of us knew where life would take us. Long before we knew we would need each other.

The Unexpected Dog

Lori Stanley Roeleveld

*The LORD is near to the brokenhearted
and saves the crushed in spirit.*

—Psalm 34:18 (ESV)

It was the worst summer of my life.

Not only was it the worst summer of my life, and my husband, Rob's, life, but it turned out to be the worst summer of my parents' lives, too.

It didn't start that way. Initially, I was excited about the warm months ahead. In mid-June, I signed a contract to write my fourth book. The project would be demanding. I had a tight deadline. My father was terminally ill but still relatively active 2 years after being given 6 months to live. My parents needed our support but lived nearby. As I stared at the calendar, I formed a plan.

If I used every moment I wasn't working my full-time day job or caregiving, I could make my deadline. There was significant research, prayer, writing, and rewriting that went into accomplishing a book of this size, but God had called me to it, so I knew He would help me keep my commitment. That faith was about to be tested.

In July, life unraveled.

First, Mom was involved in a slow-motion accident with a trailer truck. She had stopped for the truck backing onto the road but watched, horrified, as the driver just kept backing right into her car.

Her physical injuries were minimal, but understandably, she suffered severe emotional strain, especially around traveling in cars. It was too much of a challenge to drive and only a bit less stressful to be a passenger. My dad, a retired fire chief, still hadn't gotten the hang of driving a car with no emergency lights. He often forgot he didn't have right-of-way, which led to hair-raising moments at intersections. Nervous passenger and forgetful driver—not a healthy combination. I was drafted to chauffeur Mom to her numerous appointments.

I worked out intermittent family medical leave from work so I could be available when needed. This required extra work and careful planning—but no problem, I thought. God saw this coming. Families pull together. I can work full-time, provide part-time care, chauffeur Mom, and write a book, right?

The summer got worse. At the end of July, my parents' beloved pet dog, Hercules, Dad's "little buddy," lost the use of his back legs. It was clear that it was time to let him go, but with all they were facing, Dad struggled with the decision. Since Dad's diagnosis, after every medical procedure, Hercules had been waiting to comfort him as soon as Dad collapsed into his recliner. They watched television together, napped together, and even shared the occasional snack (when no one else was looking).

Throughout Hercules' last week, Dad remained in denial of what was obvious to everyone else. Mom made the vet appointment so the little guy wouldn't suffer and at last, Dad reluctantly said his final goodbye. As I lifted Hercules from his arms, grief overwhelmed him. Dad's own death loomed large, and this loss made it real. Hercules would go on ahead.

The accident, the illness, and now, the loss of Hercules put a strain on my parents' relationship. My husband and I became comforters in chief and occasional comic relief as we tried to brighten their most challenging summer. My writing time shrank, but I pressed on in faith. God would see us through. I clung to faith, but life was about to get exponentially worse.

---

*"That's him!" Dad said, suddenly animated.
"That's our dog. I want that one."*

Two weeks later, Mom and Dad were doing better together but still grieving their pup. To escape his grief, Dad decided to paint their outdoor basement entrance. It was going fine until he was hit by a sudden dizzy spell. Dad fell down the wooden basement steps to the concrete below, fracturing his spine and requiring emergency surgery. In his condition, the risks of surgery were high, but without it, he would be immobilized through what time remained.

At the same time, Mom experienced a severe bout of vertigo. My husband cared for her while I helped Dad in the hospital. There were moments when I thought my heart would explode.

Dad's surgery was successful, but he required rehab before returning home. As a fire chief for over 5 decades, he was accustomed to being in control. Now, already terminally ill and "sentenced"—as he would say—to weeks of rehab, his spirits plummeted. As his chief caregiver, Mom had her heartaches, too.

Knowing she would soon be alone, my husband talked with Mom about searching for another dog. I began looking at pet finder sites with Dad, hoping that would lift his growing depression. Visit after visit, I showed him pictures of available dogs. Initially, he had no interest. My mother was hesitant, too, and put down absolute conditions for what type of dog she would accept. Dad became convinced she would never find a satisfactory pet.

Then one day, Mom agreed to visit shelters with Rob. Dad started to study the available dog profiles a little closer. One afternoon, a shaggy dog named Lester appeared on my tablet screen.

"That's him!" Dad said, suddenly animated. "That's our dog. I want that one."

I scanned his profile. "Aw, Dad. This little guy won't work. Mom said no puppies. He's a puppy. She'll only take a house-trained dog, and this says Lester isn't trained. No way she'll go for him."

Mom wasn't one to compromise on pet requirements. Knowing there was no point in arguing, Dad lost interest in looking. Whenever I brought it up, he'd say that he'd found his dog. He only wanted Lester. I said nothing to Mom or Rob, but I did plenty of praying for Lester, or for Mom to find a loving rescue that Dad would enjoy just as much. God knew the miracle we needed.

After several weeks, Dad was able to return home. I'd written my book in emergency departments, in waiting rooms, in the rehab center, and on my parents' sofa. It was nearly done, and I marveled at God's faithfulness in helping me get through it all. But even I was surprised at God's added gift.

Rob had insisted Mom go to one last local shelter before giving up on finding the ideal dog. On the day Dad came home, once he was settled, Mom and Rob left for the shelter. While they were gone, Rob texted me to let me know that she'd found a dog she liked, and they were in the process of filling out the paperwork. A miracle! I prayed that Dad would grow to love the dog she'd chosen.

A few hours later, Rob and Mom returned with the new family member, whom Mom had decided to name Patches.

When they came through the door, my heart nearly burst. I recognized the dog. Was this Lester? I was almost certain, but it couldn't be, could it? Surely Mom hadn't loosened any of her requirements. "Isn't this a puppy?" I asked her.

"Well, yes, but he's so cute, isn't he?"

"Is he housetrained?"

"Well, no, but I couldn't leave him behind."

Leaning on his walker, Dad rounded the corner and his face lit up. "That's him! That's the dog I wanted!"

"Don't be silly. You didn't even visit the shelters," Mom said.

Dad and I just smiled. We knew. Dad put a finger to his lips, and we relished the miracle of the moment quietly between us.

Patches would go on to be a comfort to my dad in his final years, and he continued to comfort my mother when Dad was gone. An unexpected dog from a God who loves to provide unexpected answers to the prayers of the brokenhearted.

A Thread of Blue

Rhoda Blecker

*Speak to the Israelite people and instruct them
to make for themselves fringes on the corners of
their garments throughout the ages; let them attach
a cord of blue to the fringe at each corner.*

—Numbers 15:38 (JPS)

One of the projects in our congregational arts group was making our own *talesim* (prayer shawls). When our *rebbetsyn* (rabbi's wife), Bonnie, announced what we would be doing, a lot of us looked at one another, grinning. We'd been making some good and useful things recently, but this sounded like a huge step up. For me, it was a very special project.

I had been sewing since graduate school, where my apprenticeship was in costuming, and when I discovered needlepointing, I realized I loved it. So when Bonnie started leading the arts group, I had hopes for the forthcoming stitchery; Bonnie was the kind of seamstress with a separate room for the sewing machine, piles of fabrics, books about sewing techniques all over the world, and hundreds of all types of accessories. She made beautiful decorations for the synagogue, helping to enhance our experiences in the sacred space. I was especially excited about making *talesim* for me and my husband, Keith, because we had decided that we would be buried in each other's prayer shawls. It would be like we were being embraced by each other even in death.

I told Mother Miriam, my nun friend, what I was planning to participate in, and she immediately said, "Let me send you the wool for the prayer shawls." I hadn't really thought of doing them in wool, but she was so eager to be part of the project that I agreed at once. Mother Miriam's monastery was a farm, and I had participated in cattle-feeding, alpaca-walking, and sheep-bathing activities when I visited,

---

I couldn't find the light-brown needlepoint yarn. It wasn't in any of the places I expected it to be . . . it was just gone.

---

so the offer was not hugely unusual, if unexpected. Several weeks later, balls of the uneven homespun yarn arrived. Then I had to figure out what to do with it.

I'm a terrible knitter, so that was out. Bonnie suggested weaving. "I don't have any kind of loom," I said.

"There are weavers out there," she said, and when I protested that I was supposed to be making the *talesim* myself, she pointed that I would need to create the *atarot* (the traditional bands at the neck) and tie the *tzitzit* (the required knotted fringes at the corners) myself, and that would be more than enough to qualify. "Once it's woven, it's just another fabric," she assured me.

I found a weaver who was more than happy to participate and gave her the wool Mother Miriam had sent. When we discussed the lengths of the shawls, she said there wasn't quite enough wool, but she had a comparable homespun and was more than willing to contribute to the project. Her wool was a darker brown than the cream-colored wool I already had, but it was beautiful, and I decided to take advantage of the color scheme.

While she was weaving, I got a needlepoint canvas and sketched out a simple design for the band using two shades of brown silk yarn. I decided to put the logo of our synagogue (a Star of David with the upper band of the point-down triangle morphed into the top of a heart) at either end of the band, but since I really wanted the heart-star to stand out, I chose a pale blue to use for that.

Bonnie helped me set the bands on the woven *talesim,* and then there was nothing left to do but add and knot the fringes. But the strands of wool I would be using for the fringes were machine-made, much firmer and more regular than the homespun. When I thought about it carefully, I worried that the fringe wool would wear through the homespun, so I thought I'd use the lighter brown *atarah* yarn to make eyeholes in the fabric through which I could thread the fringe wool before I tied the knots.

I couldn't find the light-brown needlepoint yarn. It wasn't in any of the places I expected it to be; it hadn't fallen down behind the dresser (the customary repository of missing objects); it was just gone. Somehow it never occurred to me to use the dark brown. So I picked up the only other color I had—the pale blue I had used for the heart-star—and carefully stitched the four eyeholes in each *tallis.* They looked pretty, and that was all I cared about.

Tying the knots is a prescribed process, so I found a chart showing how to do it. After the several days it took me to get it right for the four *tzitzit* each for Keith's and my prayer shawls, I considered the project complete. The next time I went to the synagogue for the arts group, I took the two *talesim* with me to show off what I had done. In the synagogue hallway, I ran into the rabbi.

"Is that your *tallis*?" he asked. "Let me see."

I unfolded the top *tallis* and handed it to him, proud of the finished product.

He glanced over it, and then said happily, "Look, you even put a thread of blue on the corner!"

As soon as he said it, something clicked in my memory: The verse from Numbers 15 where the Lord told Moses that the Israelites should put blue thread on the corners of their garments, so that whenever they saw the fringe they would remember God's commandments. I had completely forgotten; it hadn't even entered my memory when I planned our *talesim*. But God, of course, knew exactly what He was doing.

I was still mulling about that when I got home, and by that time I had realized that I was all wrong about the *talesim* being *my* work. I had contributed to them, certainly, but they were much more of a collaboration: In addition to mine, contributions had been made by Mother Miriam, the weaver, and Bonnie, too. But when, later that night, I found the light brown thread exactly where it was supposed to be, in a place that I was sure I had looked at least three times without finding it, I had to admit that another collaborator on the project had to be God, steering me, as God always seemed to, in the proper direction.

Who in the World Is Joe Montana?

Roberta Messner

*You know when I sit and when I rise;
you perceive my thoughts from afar.*
—Psalm 139:2 (NIV)

A few years ago I hired a guy to help me liquidate my storage unit. I'd been ill and couldn't do it by myself. I hoped that if I could clear it out and cancel the rental, I'd have another $100 a month to put toward my medical bills and fixing up my old log cabin, which was falling down around me. My helper's name was Necco (named after the candy wafers he loved but rarely had). He came on the recommendation of a friend. "Really sad story," she told me. "Not much of a family. But he's the hardest worker ever."

Necco was in terrible pain from a foot injury, yet he couldn't do enough for me. As the door to my unit rolled open, he took in the vintage collectibles crammed to the ceiling from my magazine stylist days. Quilts. Lamps. Pictures. Small furniture items. It all had to go.

He let out a slow whistle at the sight. "Got any Joe Montana?" he asked.

I had just about everything, but I seriously doubted that one. "Who in the world is Joe Montana?" I said.

"You gotta be kidding. The 49ers? Greatest quarterback in the history of the good ole US of A? They say he won four Super Bowls. I say more. There's gotta be a Joe Montana ball cap or something in here."

I assured him I'd never seen Joe Montana, much less collected him. "But I'll make you a deal, Necco. If he shows up in this mess, he's yours."

"If a guy could choose his family, know who I'd pick?" Necco asked.
"Joe Montana?" I guessed.

The two of us worked long into the evening. Lots of surprises, like my mother's stoneware pitcher and Mamaw's cameo ring. But no Joe. I felt so bad for Necco. All day long, he talked about his life. It had been one bad break after another. I watched him on that ladder, determined to not drop a thing, his face grimacing with every move. The way he savored the coffee and cookies I'd gotten him. Told me he'd never worked for anyone who'd given him Oreos. Organized everything into sell, donate, and keep sections, treating it all like treasures when he had so little.

I pretended to busy myself with a stack of antique coverlets and had a talk with God. *Necco's the treasure, Lord. Not this stuff. Isn't there something here I can give him to let him know how special he is?* Life sure wasn't telling him that.

We were about to finish up when, beside a stack of embroidered linens, Necco spotted one of those big old family Bibles. It had been in a box of books at a long-ago estate sale priced for five bucks as a lot. If the three-inch-thick volume had been an ordinary title, I would've tossed it. But you can't do that to the Holy Book so I'd held onto it.

Necco was dog tired, but grinning at his prized find. The gilding stuck to his sweaty arms. "How much?" he asked. "Whatever it is, I'll work it off, Roberta." As he studied the word *family*, his eyes took on a wistful look. "If a guy could choose his family, know who I'd pick?"

"Joe Montana?" I guessed. What else? It was all he could think about.

When I dropped Necco off at his apartment, he couldn't wait to haul the huge tome inside. To give it a place of honor on the "bedside table," which he confessed was really the wood floor next to his mattress. He kept trying to pay me. I had to keep reminding him, "It's a gift, Necco. *It's yours!*"

When I handed him his money, I apologized for being close on cash. The day had gone longer than planned. "I'll find you and bring you a nice tip," I promised.

As time passed, I neither saw nor heard tell of Necco. Then one afternoon I spotted him mowing a lawn. I pulled over and fished for the bill I'd been saving in my wallet. "Oh, Necco! It's you! I have your money."

He seemed better, brighter somehow. He brushed my offering away. "I'm not taking anything else, Roberta," he said. He leaned on the sputtering push mower and let out a long whistle. Like he did when he first saw the job I had for him.

"Remember that Bible you gave me?" he asked. "The one with the two bookmarks?"

Funny, I'd never noticed any bookmarks.

This time Necco was really grinning. "Yes siree. Joe Montana rookie cards."

A thrill shivered through my body. A crystal-clear memory flashed through my mind, the estate sale vendor telling me that he'd been through every one of those books and that there was nothing of value in them. But rookie cards could be worth a lot of money if they were the right ones and in great condition. Like hundreds to thousands of dollars each.

Your cabin's in as bad a shape as you are, Roberta. Think what that money could buy. I tried to keep my voice steady, but it no was use. High-pitched sounds wobbled out of my mouth. "Did you say rookie cards? What. Kind. Of. Shape. Were. They. In?"

Necco positively glowed. "Oh, *perfect*, Roberta. They were so perfect. I put three thumbtacks in each of Joe Montana's heads to make sure they stayed on the wall."

T-t-t-thumbtacks? Mint-condition Joe Montana has three holes? In both of the cards? I was going to be sick.

Then a rustle in my spirit changed everything. Hadn't I wanted Necco to feel special? To find something in that maze of a mess meant just for him? Asked God for that very thing?

The smile that stretched across my face was as wide as Necco's. A smile that didn't come from me any more than those rookie cards had. A smile that returns every time I remember.

Make Necco feel special, Lord? That's exactly what happened.

God's Mysterious Ways: Unexpectedly Found

Some lost items can be a minor irritation, like a spool of thread you were planning to use for a project, and sometimes they can be heart-stoppers, like an engagement ring that's fallen into a muddy river. Sometimes what we're searching for isn't a lost item but something else that we need—a new friend, for example, or a canine companion.

What do you need to find in your life today? Have you thought about asking God for it?

- **Pray.** In your prayer time with God, you're probably already asking Him for the things that you're looking for and the things that you need, but consider also asking Him to show you the things you haven't seen yet.

- **Seek.** As you go throughout your day, consider the things that you find. Are they telling you something about what you need?

- **Act.** If you find something unexpected, whether it's something you prayed about or something you hadn't even thought about, hang on to it. If it's an object, put it in a special place to remind you of God's work in your life. If it's a person, nurture the relationship.

- **Reflect.** Think back on times you've found something you were sure you'd lost. Did you feel God's hand at work? Do you now?

She's Going to Be OK

Jo Ann Fore

You are the God who works wonders; You have made known Your strength among the peoples.
—Psalm 77:14 (NASB)

After a broken night of sleep stemming from an argument with my 19-year-old daughter, Tabitha, my phone rang. According to the clock, her overnight shift at the health care center had just ended. I hoped she was calling to apologize.

It wasn't Tabitha's voice on the other end, but rather that of a frantic young man, her boyfriend. He was calling to tell me Tabitha's car had flipped over a guardrail and two lanes of traffic, landing on the opposite side of the highway.

A good Samaritan, who later described the sobering moment she watched the accident unfold, had selflessly stopped. My daughter, freaking out and disoriented, her head bleeding, stumbled outside the car and repeatedly asked the stranger, "Am I going to die? Am I going to be OK?" After phoning emergency responders, Tabitha's boyfriend was called.

"There must be some mistake," I insisted. But a wave of worry and unease hit me hard, quickly followed by a strong remorse. My mind flashed to the previous night, when

Tabitha had decided she was too busy with her new friends to attend our Thanksgiving gathering. She'd canceled at the last minute, and it was the first holiday celebration she'd chosen not to attend. I was hurt, feeling like she had callously abandoned our family tradition.

It felt that way a lot recently. Seeking to assert her freedom, Tabitha made an impulsive decision to move away from home a couple of months prior. It had been a difficult and emotional time for both of us lately, and last night's decision only added to the strain.

But in this moment, none of that mattered.

"I feel sick," I whispered. As I leaned against the wall, I accidentally hit the shelf, causing the car keys to jangle loudly in the empty kitchen. *I have to get to her.* My mind racing and my body trembling, I left and headed for the quickest route to the hospital.

While making my way there, Tabitha's father called. Though divorced for years, we were still family. With a troubled voice, he slowly recounted the conversation that he'd just had with Tabitha's older stepbrother.

"On the way to work, I passed a wreck on the interstate. It was bad!" he told his dad. Although he couldn't be sure, he was worried that the car might have been Tabitha's because of a distinctive marking on the side. "The car is crumpled up like a soda can, unrecognizable except for a thin orange stripe painted down the side. I hope it wasn't her. Honestly, I can't imagine anyone made it out of there."

Tabitha's car had been a birthday gift. A compact two-door design with a pristine white exterior that gleamed in the sunlight. At first glance, it could have been mistaken for any other small white car on the road, but upon closer inspection, a subtle orange pinstripe could be seen running the length of the car. We often teased her that she'd never get away with anything corrupt in our small town with such an easily recognizable car.

A raw, gut-wrenching fear started climbing up my throat. Battling the rays of the early morning sun bright in my face, I took multiple wrong turns. The air circulating in my car felt heavy, suffocating. My mind and instincts failing me, I started to doubt my own sense of direction. In a hometown where

---

One of the voice messages was from Tabitha's stepbrother: "I'm in the room with her; she's going to be OK."

I'd spent 30 years crisscrossing all the backroads, everything familiar slowly blurred into unknowns. I was lost.

Somewhere in between where I was and where I needed to be, the phone rang again. I pulled over to the side of the road but froze, unable to answer. As the call slid into voicemail, regret flooded me. I had to know what was happening, so I forced myself to check messages. One of them was from Tabitha's stepbrother: "I'm in the room with her; she's going to be OK."

She's going to be OK. That voice on the other end was a lifeline, a connection I desperately needed in that moment. A feeling of relief washed over me like a gentle wave of warmth. As I took a few deep breaths, letting the news sink in, relishing the newfound calm bubbling up, I recognized that in my panic, I'd been aimlessly circling the same two roads that led directly to the hospital. A couple of short turns delivered me to the entrance.

Summoning my courage, I made my way inside, only to find myself at the back of a long line of people waiting for registration. And no amount of foot tapping or heavy sighing moved them through faster. Already overwhelmed with emotions, it felt unbearable, so in a split-second decision, I broke out of the line and stormed toward the double doors that led to the treatment rooms.

"You can't go back there, ma'am." With a calm but firm voice, the receptionist explained the area was restricted to authorized personnel only.

Ignoring her, I opened the door to a maze of sterile hallways, each identical to the other. Behind me, I could hear the shuffling feet and murmuring voices drawing nearer. There was nothing to do but choose a direction and start looking.

The staff caught up with me just as I caught a glimpse of my daughter lying on a stretcher in the final hallway. The area was illuminated by bright fluorescent lights, and she was surrounded by machines and unfamiliar faces.

"Mama, is that you? Am I going to be OK, Mama?"

Despite the objections of my medical escorts, I ran to her side. She looked much worse than I expected, so to keep my threatening tears at bay, I stared at the small space between her worried emerald eyes, directly above her button nose. Clasping the hand she offered, I promised her, "You're going to be just fine!"

I hoped I wasn't lying.

I walked alongside her stretcher through a chaotic but confident flow of nurses and emergency personnel. Later, they carefully sewed up the wound in her head, stitch by stitch. As the metallic scent of blood filled the air, I listened to her stifled cries.

Watching her suffer was one of the hardest things I've ever had to endure.

Finally, the sound of beeping machines faded into the background as the doctor assured me that, with an extended healing period, she would be OK. After she drifted into a medicated sleep, I made my way into a chair near Tabitha's stepbrother, one of several concerned family and friends who had finally been allowed to come and see her.

"Thanks so much for calling to let me know you were with her," I said. "My mind was a tangled mess! What should have taken me 10 minutes to get here took three times as long."

His eyes grew confused. "Ummm—I'm not sure who called you, but it wasn't me," he said. "This is the first I've seen Tabitha since I got here. They stopped us at the double doors and wouldn't allow anyone back."

My breath stalled. Emotions flooded me, from disbelief to astonishment to everything in between. Glancing downward, I managed a smile and turned away, afraid if I said anything my voice would crack.

I frantically flipped open my phone, searching for the saved voicemail. But it wasn't there. With shaking hands, I scrolled through the recent calls, hoping to find some indication he'd called. But there was nothing. I rechecked multiple times. There was no message and no sign of any kind that anyone had ever even called.

My mind raced with questions. It made no sense. *Was it a mistake? Was there a misunderstanding? Or was it something else entirely?*

I used to think miracles belonged solely to a distant era. But no amount of other explanation could do justice to what I had experienced—a moment of grace, a moment of peace, when I was desperate for it. It was as though God Himself had sent me a comforting and unignorable sign of His calming presence, reminding me I was not alone.

The Day a Lunch Meeting Provided More Than Just a Meal

Laura R. Bailey

Be very careful, then, how you live—not as unwise but as wise, making the most of every opportunity, because the days are evil.

—Ephesians 5:15-16 (NIV)

"I'll take my usual." Passing the unused menu back to the waitress, I turned my attention to my lunch meeting. This was a familiar scene; I'd been working with this client for a few years now, and talking business at one of our favorite lunch spots was a regular occurrence.

We bantered a bit, and eventually, as the plates were cleared, I transitioned the conversation to pending business matters. "Before we talk about that, do you mind sharing how you know you are a Christian?" my client asked. Lifting my eyes and dropping my pen, I struggled to gather my thoughts enough to respond.

It wasn't the first time we'd talked about our shared faith. We prayed over meals, shared various ministry events and opportunities we were a part of, and even discussed some of the current Christian hot-button issues. However, his question—the fact that he'd asked how *I knew* I was a Christian—threw me for a loop.

It should have been an easy response; I'd grown up in church, said the sinner's prayer, and was baptized at 6. So why was I struggling to come up with an answer? After a long pause, I finally stammered, "Because I accepted Christ into my heart."

His face shifted, the lines in his forehead creased, and his brows furrowed. "Yeah, but how do you know that *you* are a Christian?" he pressed again.

"Yeah, but how do you know that you *are a Christian?" he pressed again.*

Is this guy serious? Why are we even talking about this? I thought. But he wasn't giving up, so I racked my brain for a better answer. "Well, I confessed my sins and asked God to save me." I let out an exhausted sigh. Thinking that was the end, I snatched my pen and began my sales pitch again. Not missing a beat, he looked me straight in the eyes and asked a third time, "Laura, how do you know *you* are a Christian?"

The hairs on my neck involuntary rose as he asked a third time about my salvation. My mind flashed back to the Bible story where Jesus asked Peter if he truly loved Him. Jesus pressed, asking once, twice, and a third time for Peter's honest response (John 21:15–17). Unable to hide my annoyance, I spewed out, "I don't even know why we are talking about this.

You are being completely unprofessional, and I would like to start our business meeting now!"

Without blinking, he calmly responded, "No problem. But the Lord laid it on my heart to ask you. I am praying for you today."

I couldn't hide how upset I was any longer; I requested the check, waved a quick goodbye, and raced to my car. Before my hand hit the car door, uncontrollable tears poured down my cheeks. What had just happened? *Of course I'm saved; I say and do all the right stuff.* But why did I feel like something wasn't quite right?

Completely lost, I called my husband of only 6 months. I asked if he could meet me in the parking lot. When he arrived, through sobs and sniffles, I told him what had just happened. Visibly confused and caught wholly off guard, he wrapped his arms around me. "It's going to be OK."

Each Sunday growing up, I always heard the same altar call: "If you don't know that you know that you know you are a believer, make things certain today." Recalling the countless Sundays I'd heard those words as nothing more than a sign we were about to wrap up and head to lunch, I looked at my husband. "I don't know that I know, that I know."

I decided that I was going to leave work early and go home; I was too upset and distracted by my earlier conversation. I'd been wrestling with God for years. I desperately tried to outrun Him numerous times—going away to college, moving to another country, and immersing myself in work, all so I wouldn't have to deal with my inner conflict. There were weeks when I wore the mask well; from the outside, I appeared to be a put-together, if perhaps overly confident, young woman. But in the quiet of the night, I lay awake, anxious, gripped by worry and fear, unable to ignore the constant tug on my heart.

Later that afternoon, I got on my knees and cried out to God to save me. I confessed my sin and told God I was tired of fighting and needed help, the help that only He could provide. I was exhausted; I was tired of running, trying to appear put together, and believing the lie that my way was better than God's way.

My life visibly changed when I truly surrendered to the Lord—not just paying lip service to faith, but embracing a genuine heart's desire to serve God and be obedient to His will. Almost overnight, the constant noise in my head disappeared, the pounding of my heart stopped, and I began to look at life through the lens of eternity. The tantalizing little voice that accused me as I ran from God faded into the background. It was replaced with a sense of peace that I was now a child of God.

I now refer to this story as my "Damascus moment" because the Lord blindsided me with my client's question, much like he blinded Paul to save him (Acts 9:1–9). I think about that day and how God orchestrated that divine moment, all the steps, all the decisions in my life that led me to that table and that conversation.

Ten years have passed since that lunch meeting, and my life's direction has undoubtedly changed. I left my career to be a full-time mom to three little girls, went to seminary, became the Women's Ministry Director at my church, wrote a book, and regularly contribute to numerous Christian publications. One little question changed everything that day, not only for me but now also for my family, church, and community, leaving an eternal impact.

Spring Break Reunion

Jesse Neve

Many are the plans in a person's heart, but it is the Lord's purpose that prevails.
—Proverbs 19:21 (NIV)

The trip had been planned for months. My son, Jon, and his girlfriend, Rose, had everything perfectly coordinated. Jon's flight would arrive in Italy exactly 15 minutes before Rose's plane would touch down. They could each experience the happy Italian-airport reunion and then share the best spring break ever. It was almost miraculous that their spring break weeks lined up—Jon, a computer science major in Minnesota and Rose, a Wisconsin student studying abroad for the semester in Scotland. The excitement built as Jon planned and packed and purchased euros at the bank. Rose found rooms for rent and made ground transportation plans. They would explore Rome, Venice, Naples, and Pompeii. It would be a romantic Italian adventure.

And then the coronavirus crept in. We all watched the news as it spread throughout Italy. It hopped from one city to the next, and the entire country started to shut down. The couple discussed their options, and decided it was smart to move their trip to Spain. Flights and accommodations were changed. Jon would now fly in and out of Scotland, and they would make the trip to Spain together for the week. They would see Madrid and Barcelona. It would still be fantastic. Crisis averted.

And then the virus began to spread through Spain. And then the rest of Europe. Each day Jon and Rose would check the counts per country. Covid was spreading across Europe very quickly, but at that point, neither Scotland nor the United States had very many cases. From the young couple's perspective, it was just something to be avoided in certain locations, not a worldwide issue.

Since Spain seemed like a poor choice, they decided that Jon would just arrive in Scotland and they would spend their week together there, in Rose's study-abroad home of Dalkeith, which is 40 miles southeast of Edinburgh. She could show him around the places she knew and they could explore nearby new places together. At least they would get to spend some long-needed time together. They were so excited to see each other! The travel day couldn't come soon enough!

The morning of the day Jon was scheduled to depart, he left his packed bags in his dorm room as he took the city bus to his internship job in downtown St. Paul. He was planning on leaving work in the early afternoon to head to the airport for his evening flight. Rose phoned him on his way to work, and, after a very emotional conversation, they decided that it was better to call off the whole trip, in order to keep Jon safe on a continent that had very few cases of the virus at that time. There was talk of intercontinental flights being canceled, and it seemed the whole world was starting to make changes. Neither of them wanted this to be the outcome, but they both felt like it was the right thing to do. As Jon's mom, I was happy and relieved that they had come to this decision on their own, but my heart ached for them, knowing how much young love desires to be together and how excited they both were.

So Jon stayed at his internship all day instead of leaving early. We texted a bit back and forth that day, and I could tell that he was so bummed. Rose called a nearby restaurant and surprised him by having a nice sandwich and shake delivered to him for lunch. She knew that he had planned to leave early and had not brought lunch with him to work. I picked Jon up for his "spring break at home" that evening and I made his favorite dinner to try to cheer him up.

The next morning, right about the time that Jon would have been arriving in Scotland, he got a call from Rose. She was being sent home! All study abroad programs at her school were being canceled and everyone was to return to the United States as soon as possible. Jon would have arrived in Scotland just in time to help her pack up and head home. I shook my head in disbelief. How incredible is that? God knows what He is doing. He led them to make the decision to keep Jon safe at home until she could return.

Jon was able to meet Rose at the airport and they had their amazing and emotional reunion here, in Minneapolis. Not the location they were expecting, but together once again.

Never Too Late

Shirley E. Leonard

There is a time for everything, and a season for every activity under the heavens.
—Ecclesiastes 3:1 (NIV)

Did I scream into the phone? I don't remember, but I wouldn't put it past me. The lackluster day at my desk suddenly sparkled with that call from my daughter.

It's been decades now, but I still remember the lilt in Amber's voice. "You won't believe who's teaching at Montrose this year. William J. Petersen! And he's listed as connected with Fleming H. Revell."

Amber had attended the Montrose Christian Writers Conference with me for several years. In those days, I waited for the brochure to arrive in the mail, but Amber checked out the conference website ahead of time. She knew my dreams to write a book based on my years of caring for my parents. She'd listened to my stories of reading everything I could get my hands on by Catherine Marshall, whose first book was published by Fleming H. Revell.

She knew that one of my goals as a writer was to have my first rejection come from that publishing house. Now I'd have a chance to meet and talk to Mr. Petersen, who was not only a prolific Christian author but a real live editor from Revell.

I could hardly wait for conference week. But when the time came, Mr. Petersen didn't impress me at first. I was such a newbie. His class was over my head and instead of taking careful notes, I found myself daydreaming and doodling.

Yet his personality was endearing, and he invited us to call him Bill. One night after supper, as we enjoyed the rocking chairs on the porch, he asked me about my book idea. He wasn't just being polite; the subject of caregiving was dear to his heart. His mother had recently died at the age of 102, and he had cared for her before her passing. Bill looked at my notes and gently explained how far I was from being ready to submit anything. All I had in those days were the typed-up journal pages from my caregiving years.

Talking to Bill both burst my bubble and challenged me to get serious. He spoke passionately about finding the "felt needs" of the readers. This new-to-me term changed my writing life. Bill had a heart for caregivers and knew there would be a market soon, so he helped me focus my thoughts and my goals. He helped me believe I could do it. And because he took me seriously, I got a grip and kept working on the manuscript.

The year after I'd met with Bill, I sat in a class called "Author-Editor Etiquette" at the Montrose writers' conference. One of the major points made me cringe. *Always thank an editor who's helped you in any way, preferably in writing.* Ouch! It had been a year since I sat on the porch soaking up the encouragement from William Petersen. All year long, I'd picture his face and feel braver. And I'd write. And rewrite. And rearrange. And write some more. His help had been priceless, but I'd never thought about letting him know. He was a big shot. I was a nobody. This etiquette class helped me see that it didn't matter. We all need to know when we've made a difference.

I asked the editor presenting that class how inappropriate it would be to send a letter when it had been a long time. Her answer seemed simple, but I needed someone to tell me. *It's never too late to show a kindness.*

So, feeling foolish, this newbie sat down and wrote the publishing giant a letter. This is what came in the return mail on Fleming H. Revell/Chosen Books stationery:

August 6, 2001
Dear Shirley,

No, you weren't a year late with your letter. In God's timing, it was perfect.

You see, in the last few days I was wondering about the worth of a new project in which I was asked to participate. It had to do with counseling writers, and I was wondering whether I had anything of value to give or whether I was wasting my time as well as the time of others.

And then your "year-late" letter arrived. Thank you so much. Wow! I really appreciated it.

I'm sure you wondered about whether you should write after twelve months had passed, but it just proves that we need to be sensitive to God's subtle nudges.

Sincerely,
William J. Petersen

Thus began a correspondence that would span decades and humble and lift me as the work on my manuscript continued. I wrote him about every rejection (after the first one from Revell) but also about all the positive feedback I was getting from my yearly editor appointments at the July writers' conference.

The years rolled by. Bill and his wife, Ardythe, moved from Pennsylvania to an assisted living facility in Colorado. He sent me emails about caring for her. He wrote about his own journey with Parkinson's Disease. He wrote about leading Bible study and meeting with other caregivers in their new place. He wrote about singing in a chorus at 85 years of age and writing four novellas, as well as editing a comic book.

Meanwhile, I continued to pitch my manuscript to editors at Montrose. It was a new version every time. I saved my money from my job as church secretary to pay for professional critiques, and I learned so much from those. Sometimes I just met with an editor for a 15-minute free session. Eventually, that's how the answers fell into place. When my book finally found a publisher in 2012, I was thrilled to have Bill's endorsement on the back cover.

Timing is everything, they say. I had felt silly writing a year-late thank-you letter. Bill's return letter taught me a valuable lesson, and it started me down a path that ended with my book being published, helping other caregivers as Bill had helped me. God's timing is no coincidence. Is there something you've put off for too long? It really is never too late to show a kindness. Do it now.

How Crossing the Street Changed Two Lives and a Church

Laura D. Garry

Now to him who is able to do far more abundantly than all that we ask or think, according to the power at work within us, to him be glory in the church and in Christ Jesus throughout all generations, forever and ever. Amen.

—Ephesians 3:20–21 (ESV)

"Laura, are you sure about this?" he asked. The resignation letter I had pushed across the table with sweaty palms sat in front of my boss, and he looked surprised.

It took a minute for me to respond. I didn't want to disappoint my pastor and friend. Resigning from my church staff position after 17 years was a big decision, one I didn't make lightly. The church plant he started had begun with a group of friends in his living room and was now ministering to a few thousand people in a permanent space on the edge of town. I had been a part of God's work at the church since March 2001, 6 months after the first service launched in a local middle school.

"Yes," I answered. "I know it seems foolish at 50, but I sense God is leading me to go back to school. I can't juggle my current job expectations and get a master's degree if I want to immerse myself in the classes and the whole experience."

He inhaled slowly, looked me in the eyes, and asked one final question, "How do you feel as you declare your decision today?"

"I feel God's peace," I answered. In that moment the calm presence of God, the certainty that I had been waiting for, settled on my soul. Making the decision to return to school and resigning from my job had seemed risky at best. I had been wrestling with whether or not I truly understood God's leading, but the peace I felt that day propelled me forward. I connected with a couple from church who owned a law office and procured a part-time job for some income while I fully immersed myself in school. In May 2020, I graduated from the two-year program with a master's in theological studies. I couldn't have been prouder.

The Covid-19 pandemic began shortly before I graduated from school, creating the opportunity to not rush back to full-time work. Instead, I stayed part-time at the law office. I also began to investigate what it looked like to write and market a book. I had dreamed of writing a book—and as I write this, I'm currently working with an author coach to complete it. But God's plan was still in motion, and it was leading me toward a more difficult decision than any I'd faced before.

Although I had stopped working as an employee of my church when I went to graduate school, I continued to attend weekly worship there. I'd expected to stay at the church as long as my husband and I lived in the area, but throughout 2020 and 2021, I had a growing feeling that God was calling me elsewhere. I prayed long and hard about God's will for my family, and in December 2021, I exited the church doors for the last time. I kept myself from crying during the Sunday morning service, but couldn't hold back the tears as I drove home. Alone in the car, I voiced my desperate need for God to show me what He wanted me to do next.

A few weeks later, during a time of prayer, a strange idea entered my mind: starting a coffee and fellowship meeting

---

Alone in the car, I voiced my desperate need for God to show me what He wanted me to do next.

---

for friends currently disconnected from a church. One of my friends had event space downtown we might be able to rent.

I sent the friend a text message, and everything came together in record time. My husband and I began our new Sunday morning routine that January, with several other couples joining us. Typically, there were six to eight of us enjoying coffee, fellowship, and an online sermon, but only one person could join us on Palm Sunday. It was a bit disappointing to have such a small group, so the three of us decided to walk across the street from the downtown rental space and visit Central Lutheran Church.

The beautiful stone exterior of the 150-year-old structure piqued our curiosity, and we marveled at the antique stained-glass sanctuary windows. Though we didn't know anyone at the church, we felt very welcome. I subscribed to the church's newsletter, though at the time I had absolutely no idea the significance of that simple decision.

One day months later, I met a friend at a small coffee shop downtown. I shared with her how I believed God was calling me back to church work, and she encouraged me to start applying for jobs. Before I went to bed that night, I submitted my résumé online to a website geared toward helping people find jobs in ministry. I assumed finding a church staff position would require a move away from Wisconsin, where we lived. My husband agreed. It didn't seem plausible that a job matching my skills would open up at a church in our area, and my husband's job allowed him to work from anywhere in the United States.

The calendar soon flipped to August, and shortly into the month, I happened upon the email newsletter from the church we had visited on Palm Sunday. I read about the current sermon series and scanned the Vacation Bible School highlights. Then, to my surprise, the pastor's note concluded with the church's search for two full-time staff positions.

Certain my skills wouldn't meet the requirements, I opened the first job description to check. My eyes scanned the worship director title and quickly moved on, knowing my God-given talents are not musical. Imagine my astonishment when the second description for a communications director matched my skills! *God, could You be at work here?* With everything I had learned during the pandemic about writing and marketing a book, alongside my years of experience at a different church and newly acquired graduate degree, I definitely felt qualified for the position. I read the description several times, then showed it to my husband. We prayed about the job for a few days, and both sensed God's leading for me to apply. I received a call with an interview invitation, and during the interview, the pastor, church council leaders, and I were astonished at God's work to connect us. The simple decision to cross the street on Palm Sunday and subscribe to the newsletter changed my life. It would soon change another life too.

I began my new job after Labor Day, September 2022, and immediately connected to the small staff. I was excited to be a part of their team and jumped into action to execute my primary responsibilities. About a month into my new job, I

> *The simple decision to cross the street on Palm Sunday and subscribe to the newsletter changed my life. It would soon change another life too.*

was talking to a friend about the church's need to update their website. Without hesitation, she shared that another friend had a business specializing in modernizing church websites. I called the company's owner and invited him to meet our staff. The meeting went well, and we decided to move forward, so I asked for an invoice detailing the project's cost. The owner emailed me the quote, and in my thankful response, I casually wrote, "Do you know of anyone who is looking for a worship director position?" I had no idea that the question in my reply would generate a back-and-forth email correspondence that would last most of the afternoon. The sermon series at the time was titled "Asking for a Friend." I jokingly told the pastor

I was unsure if the business owner was asking about the worship director position for himself or a friend.

I didn't know the owner of the company well, but I knew he had started his marketing business alongside being a worship director at a church in a nearby town. He was the former leader of the Christian band 513FREE, and I had witnessed his musical talent at several events, including at the church where I previously worked. Unbeknownst to me, hiring him to revamp the church website was another too-amazing-for-coincidence moment. I had no clue he had been looking for a worship director position for months when I connected with him about the church website. The position had been available in the church newsletter but had not been formally posted online other than on Central's website. After a few weeks of getting to know the team, he applied for the open position and started work with the church in December.

Crossing the street to attend church on Palm Sunday 2022 began a string of God connections that changed two lives and a church. Almost a year to the day after I had first walked through the church doors, I stood alongside new friends in the midst of a packed sanctuary, celebrating Easter 2023 in a spirit of renewed hope and strengthened faith. Under the recently hired director's leadership, we all worshiped with newfound assurance that God is able to do far more abundantly than all we ask, think, or imagine.

God's Mysterious Ways: Taking Action in the Moment

Sometimes when God has a plan, He's persistent in letting you know. You feel the urging of the Spirit, or see reminders popping up all around you, sometimes in the form of attention-getting "coincidental" events. But sometimes you're confronted with a choice, or a series of quickly moving events, and all you can do is make the best decision you can in that moment. How can we make the most of those times? Are there ways to look back and get some benefit from them after the fact?

- **Pray.** In your prayer time with God, ask Him to inspire your actions so that you do just the right thing when an unexpected situation arises.

- **Seek.** Be open to new possibilities, or to questions and situations you're not comfortable with. If you encounter a challenging situation today, instead of getting frustrated, ask, "What is God leading me to?"

- **Act.** If you can see what God is leading you toward, go for it!

- **Reflect.** What are some "in the moment" situations you've encountered in the past whose purpose only became clear much later? Do you still have the opportunity to act on those later realizations?

A Cousin Connection

Ronald F. Lazenby

The LORD Almighty has sworn, "Surely as I have planned, so it will be, and as I have purposed, so it will happen."
—ISAIAH 14:24 (NIV)

"Christian Writer's Retreat," read the headline in my local church's newsletter. I was immediately intrigued. I'd never been to a writer's conference before, but the advertisement said there would be editors and publishers in attendance. I thought about the novel I was working on—a piece of biblical fiction—and the children's book I had written and illustrated for my daughter years before when she was in elementary school. *This might be a good place to pitch my projects, maybe get a contract.* I signed up.

At lunch one day during the conference, I happened to sit at a table with the instructor who conducted the classes on writing devotions. I hadn't attended any of her classes, but as we talked, she told me that her company was looking for new authors, and she encouraged me to submit a devotion for their daily guide.

Even though writing a devotion had not been on my agenda, I took her suggestion and wrote a devotion based on an experience I had the prior summer. I had been on my paddleboard in the Gulf of Mexico as an unknown 6- to 8-foot creature approached me from below. All I could see was a shadow coming toward me. Was a man-eating shark about to make me its meal? As I was making a turn to see what the shadow was, a wave caught me off guard, and I capsized—where I last saw the shadow. I had heard that sharks attack if the victim struggles, so I let myself sink several feet below the surface, remaining as calm as possible, before realizing I was not being harmed in any way. I cautiously swam to the surface and climbed onto the paddleboard. As I stood on the board and looked around, the shadow was nowhere to be seen. To this day, I do not know what it was. In the devotion, I correlated my experience of losing focus with Peter's experience of taking his eyes off Jesus while walking on the water (Matthew 14:28–31), and both of us sinking as a result.

After several edits and changes made, my devotion was finally accepted. At 65 years old, I became a first-time published author.

Unbeknownst to me, a family that shares my unusual last name of "Lazenby" was having a family reunion at the beach and read my devotion in the publication. Since we were from the same state, they questioned each other to see if anyone knew me. No one did. They figured we had to be related somehow, so one of the attendees contacted me through social media several days after the reunion to determine if and how we were kin.

When we talked, there was an immediate connection. After discussing our families' histories, we discovered his grandfather and my grandfather were brothers. He, too, is an artist; he later gave a three-day class on mixed media that I attended.

It gave us even more time to get to know each other, and we have remained close ever since. He has personally introduced me to several relatives, and through social media I have connected with other relatives I never knew I had. There are still other cousins I have not had the privilege of meeting, but I hope to at one of the reunions.

My cousin is a firm believer that there are no unimportant events for God—nothing is too small for His attention, and everything happens according to His plan. I have to agree with him. Only God could have arranged the unlikely circumstances that brought us together, from falling off a paddle board a year earlier, to attending a Christian writers' retreat and the chance meeting with a devotional editor, to uniting with unknown relatives as a result of my published devotion about the fall. As my cousin declares, "It could not have been a coincidence."

I'm Not Writing My Own Story

Sarah Greek

But as Scripture says: "No eye has seen, no ear has heard, and no mind has imagined the things that God has prepared for those who love him."

—1 Corinthians 2:9 (GW)

The early years of motherhood were rough for me. I felt like I'd lost myself completely. In that chasm, I gave up both writing and faith—too burned out for one and burned by the other. Who had energy for creativity? And betrayal seared my faith as I struggled to keep my head up in this "life I'd always wanted."

A few years into this sad sabbatical, I dawdled in the grocery store parking lot, scrolling social media and putting off going home. I stumbled across an advertisement for a young Christian women's writing retreat. I'm sure it only caught my eye because these words that would have once described me were no longer applicable.

I once would've really enjoyed that, I bitterly thought to myself. The next thought came before I could censor it: *I wish I could go.* What in the world? I chastised my brain. *I don't write anymore, or call myself a Christian anymore, and good grief, I doubt I'm considered a young woman anymore!*

I clicked the link anyway. A familiar face greeted me from the next screen. This retreat was being hosted by a Christian author I'd met years ago when I used to attend conferences—when I *was* a "young" woman—who'd had an impact on my writing. We'd connected in many ways then, and I wondered what she'd think of me now.

I want to go, my heart whispered. *You're insane!* my logic hissed. But I reached out for more information, rationalizing that maybe I'd want to go *someday*. Maybe *someday* I would want to write again.

The information I received made the whole thing seem even less obtainable: the retreat was only a few weeks away and in Colorado. I lived on the East Coast, had two kids at home, and lived on a broken budget that didn't have a "Mom's mountain retreat" column. The only upside was that I did manage to squeak into the age group they considered young women.

Then the director sent a personal note to me: "So excited to reconnect and see you interested in coming!"

I quickly wrote back that I didn't know what I was thinking and that this year was out of the question, but I'd "pray about it" for next year—even though I had no intention of doing that.

Her response was almost instantaneous: "I think you need to come this year. I think it's important. So much so that I'll write a scholarship to help cover costs if that is a concern. How much could you swing?"

I laughed out loud. "None of it! I can't afford bananas sometimes!"

To my astonishment, she wrote the scholarship for the entire tuition cost, plus room and board. If I could get travel expenses, a spot waited for me.

The emotion in the pit of my stomach was a mix of excitement, fear, and guilt. This wasn't right. There were godly women out there toiling at their writing and prayer lives, women who deserved this kind of a gift, who belonged at this retreat. Women who were not me! So why did I want this *so* much? Was I selfish enough to play someone I wasn't anymore, just for a chance to go to Colorado and have a momentary diversion from my life and kids, and have it paid for, because this author thought I was still some

---

If I could get travel expenses, a spot waited for me.

---

shining star of creative light writing God's truths? Maybe I was that selfish. But it was still impossible. We had zero money for airfare. My husband would probably pass out if I suggested leaving him and the boys to their own man-cave adventures for a few days. God knows what I would come home to!

Still, I called him anyway. He shocked my socks off, maybe even more than the scholarship message had. "I think you should go. I was just about to call you because I found out there is a special bonus on this month's check. It wasn't accounted for in the budget. If we can figure out travel expenses within that amount, I think we could swing it."

What was happening? Whose life was I living right now? I dialed our AAA agent and finally someone gave me a realistic response: "You want airfare and a rental car in just a few weeks out of small airports for a specific budget amount? That's going to be impossible." Finally, someone agreed with me. She put me on hold while I paced the floor like a caged animal. However, she came back and quoted a flight and car package that literally came within single dollars of my husband's bonus amount. I was going to Colorado!

Preparing for the retreat shook loose all kinds of identity crises. I pulled out a few dusty writing projects and felt inferiority rearing up. I unearthed my Bible, as it was on the top of the packing list, and again wondered what on earth I thought I was doing. But stretching my creativity to prepare actually felt good. I summoned the last remaining shreds of my God-believing self to attempt a half-hearted prayer of sorts that—if I was really supposed to be at this retreat—God would let me know why. I had no idea what I was in for.

When I arrived on the first day, I just stared up at the red rock mountains rising behind the conference center. Something cracked loose in my heart, and I felt alive for a minute. But more beauty was waiting for me inside as I met the other twelve attendees and felt an instant sisterhood beginning. I was seated beside a soft-spoken, beautiful soul with whom I immediately felt a connection. Her child was the same age as one of mine, and becoming a mother had been hazardous for her as well. She lived in a tiny house on wheels and, with her husband, ran a ministry of men's and women's hiking retreats in the wilderness! Part of me wanted to scoff at how her heart remained soft with her life in such upheaval, but I was fascinated by the way she lived. Even if she was completely sold on Jesus. All the women there seemed to be. I tried my best to mask this secret division between us even as their open honesty and vulnerability warmed frozen places within me. And we hadn't even started talking writing yet! I felt like I'd been starving, and this atmosphere was finally offering me sustenance.

Four of us in the group were from Pennsylvania. I'm bad at math, but it seemed highly unlikely to me that so many

Here in this mountain getaway, far from the soul-crushing life that had worn me down ... I had to make room for Him.

people from my little East Coast state would be meeting here in Colorado. I could potentially have community when I returned home from this mystical space of mountains and amazing women. If I wanted it. If they wanted me once they knew I was a fake writer and a jaded ex-Christian.

On the second night, a knock sounded on my door. I opened it to find one of the other women holding sopping towels and asking if she could room with me for the night as a pipe had burst in her room. We sat cross-legged on the bed in stocking feet as if we were having a teenage sleepover. Something otherworldly happened that night as we laughed and got to know more about each other. Her life story, which she shared openly and honestly with me, was full of outright miracles. She made connection to God seem like a living, breathing, tangible thing and not the dried-out practice I'd come to loathe. We chatted late into the night, and—honesty begetting honesty—I shared the twisting and winding story of my faith path with her. She cried; I cried. She swore there was a removal of the veil between us and God for this one night. I knew in my gut this woman before me was not lying, but speaking absolute truth. And now I had to find somewhere to put it.

I should never have been able to make it to this retreat. I shouldn't even have been interested in going. I was placed beside a woman who was swiftly becoming like a sister to me even in this short time, this new friend sleeping in my room because a leak flooded *only* her room. If I wanted to hold out and hold on to my step back from God, I had to call all these things simple coincidence. But here in this mountain getaway, far from the soul-crushing life that had worn me down, I didn't think I could do that. I had to make room for Him.

As the retreat ended, I made plans with the girls from Pennsylvania to keep in touch and keep each other writing and praying together. I talked with my new sister friend about attending one of her hiking trips—a trip that, when I took it much later, would heal many of the remaining cracks revealed by this retreat.

When I met with the director for a one-on-one session to debrief the conference, we didn't talk about writing at all. Instead, we shared about how God had curated this entire experience. She told me how many of the other woman who were so impactful for me had also been able to attend under miraculous circumstances. We surmised that God had orchestrated this entire writer's retreat to bring *me* back to Him.

Years later, as I write this story for publication, as I answer the daily texts from my closest heart friends—all of whom

I met on that trip—and as I daydream about that random three-day magical mountain time in Colorado, I still have to make room to believe. To trust that these unbelievable God moments, the way that everything came together in ways that I could never possibly have imagined, were indeed personal and planned and 100 percent nonfiction.

The Gift of a Life That Is Different than You Planned

Laura R. Bailey

*But the plans of the L*ORD *stand firm forever,
the purposes of his heart through all generations.*
—P<small>SALM</small> 33:11 (NIV)

Work was more than a paycheck; for many years, it was my identity, my reason for getting up in the morning, and the ultimate security blanket. So when I decided to leave the workforce after my second child, my new role as a stay-at-home mom took some adjusting.

For the first time in years, I didn't have anywhere to be; no one cared what I was wearing, and as long as I kept my children fed, safe, and alive, I accomplished all I needed to that day. In the following months, I struggled with finding contentment in my new routine. I joined mom-and-me groups, I made my own baby food to keep busy, and my husband often stayed with the kids at night so that I could get some adult time. But I missed traditional work, so I went back to working part-time.

My life became one of balancing my work with night-time feedings, tackling the never-ending piles of laundry, and playing Barbies until the sun went down. I loved being a mom, but I also loved working, and I felt that the two were always competing for my attention and, ultimately, my heart. However, one day, I had a conversation with a coworker that led me to take a step that would radically change the direction of my life.

Without a pause, he looked at me and said, "Just write, and don't worry about the other stuff."

My colleague shared that he had just started a blog, and I admitted that I'd recently considered writing too. He asked what was holding me back, and I confessed that I was embarrassed and worried that no one would read my writing or, even worse, criticize or make fun of my work. Without a pause, he looked at me and said, "Just write, and don't worry about the other stuff."

Unable to forget his words, I was encouraged to start writing what the Lord had laid on my heart; even if my mom was the only reader, that was OK. After a few months of late-night key tapping, I was invited to write a guest blog post by another Christian blogger. Then a few weeks later, I received another submission request, and shortly I was regularly contributing to multiple Christian publications. But the extra workload, trying to balance my job, motherhood, and writing, wore me down physically and mentally.

Rocking my daughter one morning, watching the sun peer over the horizon, I began praying. "Lord, I am scared. For the last decade, all I've known was work that produced financial freedom and security. I don't know if I can walk away completely, pursuing writing and speaking, even though I feel in my heart that's what You want me to do. I don't want to be disobedient, but I fear what the future holds; stepping out into the unknown is more than I can bear. I am asking that if You want me to leave my job, You will give me a clear sign, one that I can't ignore. I know I should trust You, but I am struggling to have faith and am pleading with You to help me make the right decision."

Hearing tiny footsteps coming down the stairs, I knew that was my sign to get the coffee going and prepare for the day with my two little girls. That afternoon, as I did every day after I got the girls down for a nap, I checked my email. There was a note from my manager that we needed to talk, and she asked that I give her a call when I had a chance.

Anxious to hear her news, I called her immediately. She shared that unfortunately, I couldn't continue working part-time, but the good news was they wanted to offer me a full-time job. As soon as she said the words, I knew I had to turn down the offer. Working full-time wasn't an option for my family. Logistically, it didn't make sense. However, I knew that there was a deeper reason to say no: this was the Lord closing a door. I politely declined. Even though I was walking away from a decade-long, stable career, I wasn't anxious. I had peace, and I was excited to see what the Lord had in store for me.

Now with a few extra hours a week of availability, I decided that I needed to hone my craft. I enrolled in a biblical women's certificate program and at the same time joined a writing group. After completing the programs, I was invited to join a well-known Christian women's ministry, writing devotions and teaching other women about the Bible. I then published a book and was given multiple opportunities to speak and encourage women with the truth of the Gospel. After a few years of studying, writing, and speaking, to my utter shock and amazement, my church asked if I would be the Women's Ministry Director.

There wasn't anything inherently wrong with my career choice or being a working mother. But the Lord had a different plan for me, one that I had never considered but was far better than the one I'd imagined. There are still days that I wrestle with my flesh; my deep desire for control and certainty can distract me from walking the path of faith. But, in His infinite grace and mercy, the Lord shows me He is in control and guides me back on course. It might be from reading a verse at just the right time, through the words of a dear sister in Christ, or even a feeling of peace only Jesus can provide. The Lord is in the details of our lives. It's not a coincidence; it's divine intervention.

The Best Mistake I Ever Made

Laura Yeager

Blessed are those who keep his statutes and seek him with all their hearts—they do no wrong but follow his ways.
—Psalm 119:2–3 (NIV)

"Hey, Mom?" I asked on the phone. "Is the Iowa Writers' Workshop in Ames or Iowa City?" I was applying to graduate schools, and I needed to know where to send my GRE test scores.

"I think it's in Ames," she said.

So began my graduate school odyssey. Of course, my mom was wrong. The famous Iowa Writers' Workshop was in Iowa City. But this was in January 1986, pre-Internet, and I would have had to make a trip to the library to look up the address.

I had graduated from Oberlin College six months before, and I was taking a year off before graduate school. At the time, I was staying with my friend Dina in New York City, and she didn't know either.

This was how my GRE scores and my grad school application ended up at Iowa State University instead of the University of Iowa. I believe the mistake was an act of God. Raised

Catholic, I certainly believed in God, and I prayed regularly and attended mass, but I'd never seen God's work in my life so dramatically until that time.

Flash forward to June 1986. It was a beautiful, sunny day. I was sitting in the family room of my childhood home in Ohio. The wind was blowing through an open window. I was reading to pass the time. I'd gone to the library and checked out the most recent O. Henry Prize collection. The short story I was reading was entitled "Lily," by Jane Smiley. I'd never heard of her before, but I was extremely impressed with the story, and wasn't surprised to learn that it had tied for first place that year.

Now comes the best part of my story.

The very next day, I received a letter in the mail from Iowa State University. I opened it and read the typed missive. I had been accepted to the creative writing program, and not only that, but the school was also offering me a fellowship—The Pearl Hogrefe Fellowship, consisting of full tuition and a living stipend.

The letter was signed by Jane Smiley.

Now this, my friends, was miraculous to me. I remember screaming throughout the house that Jane Smiley had personally written me a letter.

"Who is Jane Smiley?" my mom asked.

"She's a famous writer who offered me a full fellowship to ISU!"

Mom and I held each other's hands and jumped up and down.

That fall, I loaded up the old family station wagon and moved myself to Ames, where I lived and studied for 2 years.

Those 2 years were the best of life. I was out on my own, single, and living in farm country. I remember taking long walks around enormous corn fields, and I actually lived next to a peanut farm. Those 2 years were full of growth and happiness, and I got to study with Jane Smiley, the Pulitzer Prize–winning novelist, and other teachers who taught me everything they knew about writing. I spent my weekends going square dancing and playing volleyball with other students. What can I say? It was a wholesome and educational experience.

I have often felt that sending my GRE scores to the "wrong" school was the best mistake I've ever made. At Iowa State, I received a graduate assistantship the second year I was there and took several teaching methods classes, which helped me get teaching jobs after graduate school. Without the Iowa State experience, I probably wouldn't have been employable as a teacher after college.

Ironically, after graduating with an MA from ISU, I did end up attending the University of Iowa, so in my time in graduate school, I experienced the best of two worlds. At the Writers' Workshop, I studied with James Alan McPherson, and he too taught me so much about life and writing. My MA and my MFA degrees have served me well.

I'm now 60 and have been a writer and a writing teacher throughout my life. All I can say is thank God for His amazing works. They may be disguised as chance, serendipity, or coincidence, but they are truly the embodiment of God's love.

The Turn Around

Sohani Faria

Trust in the LORD with all thine heart; and lean not unto thine own understanding. In all thy ways acknowledge him, and he shall direct thy paths.
—Proverbs 3:5–6 (KJV)

I stared at the herd of goats, with their black-striped faces, frolicking happily in their pen. The barking of excited dogs and cheery greetings of parents picking up their kids from spring camp interrupted my musing. I was sitting in my car, waiting to pick up my daughter from Hazelmere Farms in British Columbia, Canada, a few miles from the US border.

I was a stay-at-home mom to two teenage daughters with a hard-working husband. It should have been the perfect recipe for a contented, happy life. Yet I felt empty and incomplete. Time was ticking, waiting for me to accomplish something, and I didn't know what it was. This feeling surfaced occasionally, silently crying to be heard and acknowledged, but I never understood it. Secretly, I was afraid to find out what it really was and give it a name, because the possibility that it was something that could not be fixed, that it's too late, made me shy away from delving further. *Lord, why am I not content? Why do I feel like I'm on a highway going nowhere?*

I gave those thoughts the customary dismissal. Over the years I had mastered the art of burying these recurrent thoughts and feelings under a flurry of endless mom duties and church volunteering activities. But exactly one year later, on the way to that same camp, God would answer my questions in a way I couldn't ignore.

I was driving on Highway 99, the usual route to the farm, with Liya in the back seat, listening to the familiar children's stories of the Adventures in Odyssey audio books—our favorite since my kids were tiny tots. We had done this 45-minute drive to the farm so many times.

"Mom, wasn't that our exit?" Liya suddenly said from the back seat. I had been so engrossed with the audio narration that I missed the exit for the camp.

"Oh, we can take the next one," I said, unperturbed.

But strangely, and to my dismay, I missed the next exit too. And the next, and the next. *What is wrong with me?* I wasn't *too* concerned, as I was very familiar with the landmark for the next exit—the Pink Hotel, a fond name given by those in the community because the building was painted pink. But still, I was paying careful attention, to be sure not to miss it. I gasped a minute later as I passed a huge white building on my right and realized, too late, that it was the Pink Hotel, now inexplicably painted white. I had missed the exit again!

I tossed the GPS to Liya. "Plug it in quickly," I called in a voice one pitch higher than normal, trying to stay calm.

"No street level information for this city," the composed voice of the GPS system calmly announced. I stared at it in disbelief. I had used this GPS countless times to drive in this area. A surge of anxiety went through me as I saw the signs for the US border splashed across the signposts.

There was one more exit before the border crossing.

Beach Road Exit 500K.

Saved.

I was about to exit off the highway when I saw another sign: *Exit Closed*

This cannot be happening to me.

I was horrified when it finally dawned on me: I was about to go through the Peace Arch Border Crossing and enter the USA with only my driver's license and no ID for Liya. I was a person of color married to a European, and my daughter looked nothing like me. Her skin tone was so light. In my frazzled state of mind, she seemed to have gotten two shades lighter since this morning and my hands, gripping the wheel, seemed to be two shades darker. And now that she'd realized she was going to be late for camp, she was clearly unhappy—that wouldn't help my case with the border officers, either.

There was no turning back. I was so flustered I accidentally swerved into the Nexus lane, which was reserved for pre-screened travelers holding special cards for express travel between Canada and the United States. I had just doubled any penalty I would receive.

There were only a few vehicles ahead of me, and then it was our turn. My heart sank as I silently prayed for God's mercy.

"ID, please," said the border officer.

I held out my driver's license.

"Where is her ID?" he said, nodding in Liya's direction. "And the Nexus cards?"

"I'm so sorry, but I missed my exit. I wasn't planning on crossing the border," I said, keeping it a singular "exit," as I was too embarrassed to say I had somehow missed five of them. "And I don't have any ID for her. She's my daughter."

"Are you aware of the penalty for trying to enter a country with a child who has no ID? Why did you use the Nexus Lane without a Nexus card?" The questions were fired at me while she punched in my driver's license number on her computer.

I was certain that everyone within a 1-mile radius could hear my heart thumping.

My car was tagged with a red sticker and I was asked to drive slowly to a building on the left.

Will they separate Liya from me? Will they ask for her dad's contact? What if they can't reach him? We stood in line while my mind churned out the worst-case scenarios, and then it was our turn.

"Mom, can I text Sydnee to send you a picture of my ID?" Liya said, emphasizing the "Mom." She had clued in to the danger of our situation, and purposely spoke loud enough for the officer in front of us to hear. But when she texted, there was no reply from her older sister at home. I had been ready to offer unlimited TV time and anything else she demanded to send us that picture.

After more of the same questions from the border officer and more stammered answers that sounded suspicious even to my own ears, suddenly he seemed to realize I was telling the truth. I marveled at God's power to suddenly change a dire situation in favor of His children. This could have turned ugly.

"I'm going to open this gate," he told us, leading us outside. "Turn around here and head right back." I silently thanked

God as I did a U-turn and headed back to Canada. My relief was short lived as I faced the Canadian border. *How do I prove she is a Canadian citizen?*

Suddenly, I remembered that her medical card from yesterday's doctor's appointment was still in my jacket pocket. Why hadn't I remembered it when they asked me for her ID card at the US border?

It took less than 2 minutes for the Canadian border officer to believe my story. He waved us away, shaking his head, probably thinking, *How could she have missed five exits?* Even I couldn't believe what had just transpired. I had driven to the

---

Strangely, and to my dismay, I missed the next exit too. And the next, and the next. What is wrong with me?

---

farm countless numbers of times and had missed my exit on a rare occasion but had never ended up at the US border.

"Exit right in 600 meters," the GPS suddenly said, making me jump. Just 20 minutes ago, at this same spot, it had informed me there was no street level information. Though I couldn't quite understand what was going on, I suddenly had a sense that the Lord was with me. I was engulfed by a deep sense of peace.

Twenty minutes later, Liya had joined her spring camp group, and I drove to a quaint café nearby. Armed with a blueberry muffin to calm my nerves, I sank into a chair and settled in to wait while she finished her camp.

As I tried to process what had just happened, the atmosphere in the café changed. The chatter in the coffee shop, the whir of the coffee machine, everything just faded into the background. In that quiet space I simply knew, inexplicably, that the Lord had used that forced turnaround to speak to me. I understood that God was drawing a parallel between what had just taken place and my life. I felt Him saying I had missed His spiritual exit signs because I was too busy ticking off items on my "good-girl to-do list." I was rushing along a highway of my own making. My busy life was hiding purposelessness and many deep hurts that needed healing.

I felt overwhelmed by a strong conviction that He wanted me to start writing. I loved to write, but I had never taken it seriously or invested time or effort to hone this gift. My thoughts flashed back to pastors, friends, and family encouraging me to write. I did, but it was done frivolously: lighthearted poems for someone's birthday, letters of appreciation to my children's schoolteachers, and Facebook posts when I felt like it. I had categorized it in my mind under "do when you have time." *How could I have missed all those clues?*

Sitting there in that little café, I felt a stir of excitement mixed with doubt and hopelessness. I was middle-aged now, and the fear that it might be too late began to creep in. Questions of where to even begin, plagued my thoughts, threatening to crush the glimmer of hope that desperately tried to surface.

I left the café with such peace and joy—but also with a whole lot of questions on my mind—and drove to pick up Liya. Our drive home was peaceful and uneventful.

The next morning, I braced myself to accomplish as much as I could on my to-do list and guiltily grabbed my Bible, knowing I had only 5 minutes before the school rush. As I flipped it open, my eyes were drawn to a scripture in Jeremiah: "Set thee up waymarks, make thee high heaps: set thine heart toward the highway, even the way which thou wentest: turn again, O virgin of Israel, turn again to these thy cities" (31:21, KJV).

A chill went up my spine. There was no mistaking it. He was confirming what He had said to me the day before. I was

---

In that quiet space I simply knew, inexplicably, that the Lord had used that forced turnaround to speak to me.

---

spellbound that the Creator of the universe was speaking to little old me. Me. A stay-at-home mom with no career, no direction, going through the motions of life like a robot.

Since that day at the café, I have struggled to let go of lifelong habits of procrastination and doing my own thing. But it has not all been a waste. During this time, the Lord has been digging up the fallow ground in my heart, giving me hope to believe that He is able to restore lost time, that it's never too late to turn around and find the start line. It took me this long to bury my regrets, forgive myself for missed opportunities, and lament over lost time. He made me understand that it's not so much about the writing, but more about becoming the person He wants me to be—unashamed and confident, courageous enough to give the world a glimpse of the real me. There are days, sometimes turning into weeks, where my mind habitually looks for ways to fill my time with activities, and I find myself darting off on a rabbit trail. Then the whisper of His Spirit draws me back gently, encouraging me to sit and be still. Those times of straying have gotten shorter and shorter over the months as I learn to accept His mercy and grace each morning, letting go of the failures of yesterday, and striving to live in His promise.

One year after that pivotal experience at the border, I found myself sitting in the same car, at the same farm, once again waiting to pick Liya up from camp. But this time my heart was filled with wonder and excitement. I feel so grateful to serve a God of a second, a third, and a millionth chances. His relentless love does not rest until He brings a wayward child to a path that leads back to His perfect will—even if He has to turn her around in the most literal way possible.

God's Mysterious Ways: A Calling in Life

Do you believe that everyone has a purpose in life? Do you believe *you* have one?

The idea of purpose, or a calling from God, can sound big and important. Life-changing, if not world-changing. But as the authors in this volume might tell you, sometimes finding your purpose is just a matter of understanding where you need to be to help the people who need it most—including yourself. Whether it's being a parent, having a career, or expressing your creative vision, you never know when you're having an impact that can change someone's life forever.

- **Pray.** Are you not sure what your purpose is? Or, if you believe that you do, are there other questions that you have about it? If so, talk to God about it during your prayer time.

- **Seek.** What in life makes you happiest? When you're in the midst of that activity, notice how it makes you feel. Does it feel like purpose?

- **Act.** Do something today that aligns with your purpose in life.

- **Reflect.** What is your purpose in life? Whether you're sure you know what it is, think you might, or have no idea at all, try writing about it, and see what realizations might come from that.

Saved by a Dream

Ingrid Skarstad

Behold, I send you out as sheep in the midst of wolves; so be wise as serpents and innocent as doves.
—Matthew 10:16 (RSV)

When I was in my twenties, I was naïve. My pastor's wife, expressing concern one day, shared Titus 1:15 (RSV): "To the pure all things are pure, but to the corrupt and unbelieving nothing is pure; their very minds and consciences are corrupted." I didn't see the warning in the last half of the verse.

In a series of shocking revelations, I learned that my husband, the man I had trusted and been married to for 13 years, had been engaged in criminal behavior. I initiated divorce proceedings, and my kids and I launched our new lives without him. My new aim as a mother was to help my children, ages 12 and 5, experience joy in a hard time of change.

We sold our 1960s house with the big backyard and swimming pool and moved into a brand-new apartment with a massive pool that we didn't need to maintain. The kids didn't know what "subsidized housing" meant or that I could barely feed them. All they knew was that there were tons of friends and a great place to play.

We managed somehow. There were days when adventure and laughter broke through. There were days when dreams were dim. But I kept as much stability as I could for the kids: church and family. We knew we had each other.

One day a coworker asked when I planned to start dating. I had no plans. Surely if there was a good man in my age range, he would already be married!

She disagreed. "There might be someone in the same boat as you!"

"Maybe? But I really doubt it." I had to think about it before I could agree. Hope sprang up anyway. I didn't look for anyone, but I opened my heart. *A good man could be suddenly single because of his spouse, right?*

A first foray into the world of dating quickly turned to talk of marriage—then fell apart as counseling revealed that he was afraid to be a father to my kids, the one thing that mattered most. We parted ways, and I went back to managing our day-to-day existence. But my youngest, who had been deeply attached to the man she thought would be her new father and his family, struggled with the dissolution of the relationship. She begged me to date someone—anyone! She felt vulnerable and embarrassed that she "didn't have a family."

I turned to online matchmaking, something I had previously considered and then rejected. How can you know a person's heart based on his online profile? But I wanted to give my children a true, secure family.

From the safety of my computer, I shopped and sorted for weeks. One man stood out from the rest. He lived in a large city only 2 hours away—currently overseas working on shipping logistics for his import business. We emailed. We texted.

We spent hours on the phone discussing the Bible and family. He wooed us with gifts for my children and flowers for me. Sometimes bouquets were accompanied by chocolates or jewelry. I secretly began to swoon, and my daughter was over the moon.

For a kid who grew up without much of a dad, this man's attention fed her heart. Gifts became bigger and better. When an iPod arrived, it seemed to seal the deal. She was ready for her mom to get married when he got back to Oklahoma!

The wealth and handsomeness of the businessman attracted me. I liked business strategy and thinking big. He was a few years older than me and looked like a polished cowboy. I longed to talk with him face to face, but his video camera never worked. Instead, photos with exotic cars fed my imagination.

Just as Mr. Business was finalizing flights home, he ran into trouble. His containers had been detained in customs—something about taxes or fees. Could I help? He promised to pay me back many times over and had his lawyer draw up a contract. I didn't have the money, but my dad did, and he signed the contract.

Of course the request for money should have been a red flag, but my trusting heart didn't have a clue—not until the dream.

One night I dreamed that Mr. Business and I were in a huge building that seemed like an airport crossed with a cruise ship. We looked for each other amid an astonishing number of people. Even after I spotted him, it was nearly impossible to make my way through the crowds to where he was. He had not spotted me yet, but I could see him looking. I fought through a maze of other travelers, sometimes losing sight of him and re-navigating again. A few times, we were close enough that we could have reached each other if only our eyes had met before one of us was swept away.

I finally caught up to him on a raised landing. He was still looking out over the sea of people, intently searching. I called his name and approached. His eyes glanced through me, passing over my face to scan the crowd again. He didn't recognize me!

I turned to online matchmaking, something I had previously considered and then rejected. How can you know a person's heart based on his online profile?

I woke with a start.

This wasn't an ordinary dream. I had experienced dreams like this before, both real and surreal, that felt unexplainably different and made me want to hide in God until I could breathe again. I had more than one about my former husband, and about the man I had almost married. At the time, I had thought they were just bad dreams and stuffed them deep down inside me, far away from my waking mind. I felt horrible for having the capacity to experience them. But those dreams had come true! Maybe God had sent them to warn me. Was he trying to warn me again?

This time, I pressed in and researched everything I knew about Mr. Business. I kept my cool and played Nancy Drew, my favorite childhood detective. When I used Google Earth to look up his address, the location was suspicious. I couldn't find sufficient information about his business. I tracked the IP addresses from emails—Nigeria, not London. His lawyer didn't exist—not as a lawyer at least.

The fake lawyer had been scammed too. His life savings were siphoned away, and he was trying to recoup his money by joining the game and playing a role in the vast network. Could I help? He needed to pay his rent.

Absolutely not!

I offered instead to help him uncover and report every connection he knew. He accepted, and we milked it as long as we could. We gathered contacts, reported scammers, and intercepted innocent people. We didn't recover our money, but we came out with a clean conscience knowing we pursued justice and hopefully saved others.

The handsome cowboy whose photo had so intrigued me had been a victim too, his information harvested for a fresh profile. The dream was right—he truly didn't know me. But the Holy Spirit knew!

Yes, I missed red flags—again. But with the Lord's help, I became wiser. If I hadn't stopped and paid attention to that dream, if I hadn't followed where the trail led, I might have lost a lot more money, and lost out on the opportunity to help others avoid the same fate. Along the way, I learned that sometimes listening to God's voice means paying attention to my dreams.

Easter Moon Rising

Jennifer Clark Vihel

I have come into the world as light, so that whoever believes in me may not remain in darkness.
—John 12:46 (ESV)

It was late, three minutes past midnight, when I finally crawled into my bed. This day had been long and hard. I had just baked a chess pie to take to my church's Easter breakfast—probably the last pie I would ever bake in my beloved kitchen. I was facing divorce, the loss of my home, and a bleak, uncertain future. My drastically reduced finances—our joint monies now split in half—would not allow me alone to keep the property I had spent the past 27 years making a home. Who gets divorced after 43 years of sharing life? I had been ready to enjoy retirement with a life partner, sitting in a rocking chair on my deck overlooking the forested beauty that surrounded us. Now that dream now would never come to fruition.

Physically exhausted and emotionally weary, I pulled at my covers, rolled onto my right side, then buried my head into my pillow. Unshed tears pooled in my eyes.

I had really wanted to make that pie. But that late-night effort, along with all the added stress, had triggered my always-lurking chronic fatigue syndrome, and my body had begun the familiar shutdown I so resented. I could barely move now; yet I faced an early rise if I wanted to get to the church breakfast on time. I knew no one would go hungry if my pie wasn't there, but right now I needed my efforts to matter. So much lately, it appeared, had not.

The tall wall of windows I now faced beside my bed allowed me to look into the dark forest landscape and beyond. California coastal redwoods, fir, and spruce trees surrounded me with their silhouetted shapes. In the far distance, on a hill rising above the other trees, I spotted the lone form of a large tree with full branches and a tapered top. I stared dully at it now, ignoring the pull of its distant beauty, while allowing instead an unsatisfying numbness to overtake me.

My personal prayer ritual before I sleep was first to express gratitude to God, then to offer up prayer requests. Thoughtful gratitude seemed to set the right tone for me to further interact with my Lord. But tonight, no nugget of gratitude materialized in my mind. I was sad—so sad—and overwhelmed by the unknown to come. I feared tonight I was losing the battle to bring my thoughts into captivity to God.

I felt depleted. And defeated. I stared numbly into the darkened emptiness.

Then something remarkable happened. From behind that most distant tree, beginning at root level, I saw a bright glow emerge. At first, I feared it might be a forest fire, a genuine danger for our area. I watched closely as the glow backlit the tree's trunk, then slowly climb the entirety of the trunk's height until the fiery orb broke free, now with its glorious light hanging high above the peak of the tree!

This was no fire, I realized, but instead a late moon climbing higher and higher. Light shone down on the darkness below, changing everything and briefly offering clarity. I could see bare ground. I could see the forest floor. I could see through tree branches to the light beyond. The sight was amazing! An Easter moon was rising, and unfolding in front of me was a parallel enactment of Christ's resurrection with His everlasting light shining into the darkness of the world.

"And on the third day, He rose . . ."

Today was the third day. And Jesus's resurrection—the ultimate reason for mankind's gratitude—was on display. The symbolism was not lost on me. I was changed immediately, filled with renewed gratitude for this greatest gift.

This was no coincidence. The gift of this experience felt personal. I am convinced that I was brought to the window at just the right time to see this beautiful vision because I so badly needed to see it.

In all my years of living on this property, I had never witnessed such a spectacle. If I had gone to bed at my regular bedtime, I would not have seen it. Or, if I had gone to bed just 5 minutes later, it would have been over before I even settled. But it did happen, and because I saw, I was renewed, filled with gratitude and assurance, and once again able to smile.

That night I slept like a baby cuddled in loving arms.

Picture Perfect

Roberta Messner

*For he shall give his angels charge over thee,
to keep thee in all thy ways.*

—Psalm 91:11 (KJV)

I would never write another story again. A side effect of my medication had wracked every system of my body, taken a toll on my soul. After four decades, this *Guideposts* magazine photo session would be my last. For 6 months, I'd been so weak, I was barely able to walk from my bed to a chair. I had reached an all-time low.

The joy of creativity had once made me feel alive and at one with the world. For the past 4 decades, I'd loved telling stories of faith and hope and of the many earth angels who graced my path. The spark in my spirit was now gone forever. There were surely no angels in sight. I'd packed up my dreams in Rubbermaid tubs and relegated them to the attic.

A story I'd written about the isolation and loneliness of that time was coming out soon in *Guideposts*. They needed some pictures and a video to go with it. When Katie in the photo department telephoned to go over everything, I couldn't imagine a plight worse than a photo shoot. I awakened in the middle of the night more despondent than ever and drafted an email to cancel out. When I tried to hit *SEND,* though, I heard Katie's cheery voice in my head. *"The photographer we're thinking of is really great, Roberta. Been everywhere. Done everything. So nice, too."*

When you're in the shape I was in, the idea of working with a renowned photographer can scare the stuffing out of you. But that little word *nice* made my heart turn a flip-flop. It immediately brought to mind all of the wonderful readers who had become like an extended family to me.

I recalled the time Marla down in Galveston, Texas, had picked up on a comment I'd made in a devotional. I'd written, "I'll believe it when I see it." Marla didn't waste a second penning a different take: "You'll *see* it when you *believe* it, Roberta." Instead of dotting her i's, she drew tiny hearts over the letters. Then she added, "And if *you* can't believe just yet, *I'll* do the believing for you." She helped me see my situation could—and would—change, bless her heart.

My *Guideposts* readers were an incredible web of connection and caring. If I couldn't go through with the shoot for myself, somehow I had to do it for them.

When Scott, the photographer, called for directions, I assured him it was easy to find. "Turn off Third Avenue at 18th Street," I told him. After I hung up the phone, I heard myself say out loud: "Why didn't you tell him the truth, Roberta? I'm at the corner of hopelessness and despair." I blew my bangs out of my eyes and poured myself a bracing cup of Red Zinger tea. *Pull yourself together, Roberta.*

The morning of the shoot found me weaker and more discouraged than ever. Katie had suggested bringing in some props to make the photos come alive. There weren't enough props in this world to help my despondent mood. The gloom so showed on my face I couldn't even bear to look in the mirror anymore.

As Scott unloaded his equipment, he was already focusing on the details, combing every nook and cranny for objects to round out the shoot, curious about their origin, putting them together in inventive ways. He reminded me a little of the Roberta I used to be. But all I could focus on was making sure this photo shoot didn't drag on too long. Surely we'd be done in a couple of hours so I could go back to bed and pull the covers over my head.

But as soon as Scott positioned me at a desk with my hands resting on a stack of books, he stopped everything and stood gazing out the window, seemingly transfixed. What in heaven's name? It was an ordinary, dirt-splotched window. *Let's get this show on the road,* I inwardly grumbled.

Finally, in a hushed voice, he uttered the most astonishing words. "Along came a spider . . . and sat down beside her."

What had caught his attention was a spider's web, spread across the window with the spider's artistry on full display. I was so surprised to see him mesmerized by an ordinary spiderweb and I found myself leaning in for a look myself.

"Isn't it lovely, Roberta? It's like *Charlotte's Web*," I heard him say.

A shiver went down my spine as the memories began to flood back. *Charlotte's Web* had been my favorite childhood book. All at once, I was eight years old again. In my mind's eye I saw my mother slide the glass on our oak barrister bookcase and reach inside her once-upon-a time shelf for something she'd been saving for years. It was a storybook that had been published in 1952, before I was born. When she had learned she was expecting me, she would sit in the old platform rocker and read it out loud to me in the womb.

Charlotte's Web!

That afternoon she gave me the book to read. I'd taken Mother's prize to my very favorite place, under the big, shady maple tree in our front yard. As I leaned against its rough trunk, I discovered for the first time how a story could be a girl's best friend. When I told Mother about it, she wrapped

---

There weren't enough props in this world to help my despondent mood.

---

her arm around my shoulder: "There's *nothing* like a *story*, Roberta. And you know what? Sometimes when we're talking, I think you weave them yourself. Just like *Charlotte's Web*."

The next day Mother came home from teaching school with a tablet tucked inside her purse. Its sky-blue cover said, "My First Scribblings." That day, with my chubby red pencil in hand, I became a writer.

The photo shoot lasted for hours, but I began to lose all track of time as I began spinning stories again. For one of the pictures, Scott had me stand with my eyeglasses in my hand. "You look like a professor," he mused as he looked through the camera. Then he said something about a "daughter."

And just like that, my mind linked two words that didn't go together. *The professor's daughter.* A new energy coursed through my veins. *You never wrote about the professor's daughter.*

My connections were making connections!

While Scott set up the video, I grabbed the first scrap of paper I could find, a brown paper sack from a nearby trash can. Imagining a reader encouraged by a story, I was that once-upon-a-time girl who scribbled in a tablet. The girl who believed in happily-ever-afters.

Beside my words, I drew the spiderweb Scott had seen when he paused at the window to wonder. And I remembered another sharp detail his eyes had picked out. "Look, it's missing a few of its links."

His words filled *me* with awe and wonder. I couldn't stop thinking about the links in my own web of connection that could be broken if I stopped writing. *If you quit, Roberta, the connections with your readers will be broken,* God whispered. *To your creativity. Your calling.*

After my story was published in *Guideposts,* a reader confirmed the amazement of that photo shoot. "When I turned to the loneliness story," a woman wrote, "I knew the author's face was going to be lined with trials. Whoever took that picture put hope in it."

Actually, my angel photographer put hope inside of *me*. Every now and then I take another look at that photo myself. Remember how I came home from the shoot, headed straight for those Rubbermaid tubs. Unpacked my abandoned writing dreams and came alive. No longer dying inside because I couldn't create.

I've never stopped telling the stories God places in my path. Five years later, that picture is still worth a thousand of my words. It wasn't too late to be what I might have been. Hope was the best prop of all.

God Knew What I Needed

Rebecca Hastings

And my God will supply all your needs according to his riches in glory in Christ Jesus. Now to our God and Father be glory forever and ever. Amen.

—Philippians 4:19–20 (CSB)

Having a newborn baby is full of unknowns. How much will he sleep? Is he eating enough? Is this normal? Even though this was my second baby, I asked myself all of the usual questions. Things took a turn when he got sick.

I didn't know what was wrong, but I knew something wasn't right. Days of projectile vomiting led to doctor's visits and after-hours calls. I felt like I was at the end of my rope, unable to help my little boy. Then the unexpected came.

I was on my way to somewhere no parent wants to go. After another doctor's visit, the pediatrician sent me to the children's hospital with my three-week-old son. He wanted us to go in to rule out a blockage called pyloric stenosis. The doctor seemed so sure of himself when he said, "It's just precautionary. I think he is fine." But something in me felt this would be different.

Leaving the pediatrician's office, I loaded my 18-month-old and my 3-week-old into the minivan. I had no idea what to do as we headed to the hospital. Grocery shopping was challenging enough with two little ones. How could I possibly handle this? I knew that emergency surgery was a possibility. And I was on my own.

My husband was working in an emergency room in another town. As I drove away from home toward the city, I couldn't help but think about how alone I was. Everything in me wanted to turn around and go home, but that wasn't what my baby needed. Clutching the steering wheel as I headed to the city, I wanted to pray, but I didn't know what to say.

As much as I wanted my prayer to be for my son, my fears drowned out every other thought. The typical unknowns of motherhood were replaced with new ones. What if he needs surgery? What will I do with my daughter while my son needs tests? How could I possibly do this on my own?

Finally, my prayer took shape and I uttered the only words I could think of: "If I can't do this alone, let me run into my mom." The words came out of nowhere. It was the prayer I didn't even know I needed.

The chance of seeing her at the huge city hospital was minimal. She was supposed to be there for an earlier appointment, but she had no idea I was coming. I had tried calling, but I hadn't been able to get ahold of her. My prayer was all I had.

I pulled off the highway and around the city block. When I pulled into the entrance, my mom stood right there! She was waiting at the curb outside for her car. We locked eyes and

I knew I was not alone. God had heard my prayer, and He answered in the way I needed most. God knew I would need someone to walk alongside me.

She was as shocked to see me as I was to see her. So many things needed to line up perfectly in order for us to meet. Her appointment was supposed to be over much earlier but there was a delay. When she finally got outside there was a long line at the valet to get her car. And there she was at the exact moment I arrived. If she hadn't been delayed or the line at the valet had been shorter, we would have missed each other completely.

I explained what the pediatrician said and why we were at the hospital. Without a moment's hesitation, my mom helped me with my kids and led us inside. She carried my burden with me. Her presence strengthened me to face the unknown.

I wasn't alone. My mom comforted me and kept my daughter busy as I took care of my son. When the doctor performed the ultrasound and confirmed that my son would need emergency surgery, I was terrified, but I wasn't alone.

My son was rushed to surgery and the blockage was repaired. He made a full recovery and went home within 24 hours. But the lesson of faith I learned lasted much longer.

Until the End of the Week

Nancy Shelton, as told to Marci Seither

The LORD will guide you always; he will satisfy your needs in a sun-scorched land and will strengthen your frame. You will be like a well-watered garden, like a spring whose waters never fail.
—Isaiah 58:11 (NIV)

I gathered up library books that needed to be returned when we drove into town and checked to make sure my grocery store list was in my purse.

"OK, kids," I hollered up the stairs. "We need to get going!" The phone rang and I put the book bag down to answer it while the kids started making their way down the stairs.

"Hello?" I said into the receiver.

"Hey Nancy," my husband's voice said in a calm tone. I looked at my watch. I knew Todd took a lunch break while working his job at the local community college, but he seldom called home to chat unless it was something important.

"What's up?" I replied. I could see that all four of the kids were in the car and ready.

"I just checked the bank," he said. "We are really close to the bottom of our account, so whatever you do, don't spend anything from our checking until next payday."

I knew things were getting tight, but had hoped that Todd would have had a new job by now. He had sent his résumé out, and it felt like we were just waiting for something, anything, to open up.

"No worries," I told my husband. "The freezer is full, and we can skip on extras for the time being."

I tried to sound optimistic, but mentally I crossed things off the grocery story list that were more "want" items than "need" items. I thought of the limited amount of cash I had in my wallet plus the loose change that clinked around in the bottom of my purse.

We had felt such peace over leaving the church where Todd was the youth pastor and I was the pianist. Todd had his part-time job, but leaving the church meant also giving up both of our incomes.

Should we have stayed longer? Our financial issues made me question our decision briefly, but I knew we had made the right choice at the right time. I had grown up with a strong faith and knew God could answer prayers, but now I needed to trust Him with our basic needs.

One of our needs had already been met—to find a new church family where our kids could thrive and where we could find a place to serve. The first Sunday we slid into the pews and heard the choir at our new church, I felt at home. Soon I was singing with the choir, and I loved seeing that they had a choir for our kids as well.

"Hey, folks," said the music minister one Wednesday evening at practice, "Our pianist is getting ready to leave for a new job, so we will be shifting a few of the musicians around every other week to fill that gap until we can hire someone to take his place."

I had told the director when I joined the choir that I had been a pianist for years, so I was surprised that he didn't ask me to help out.

"I totally forgot you mentioned it!" he said when I reminded him. He asked if I could play the following week, with the plan that I would play every other Sunday until a permanent pianist could be hired. Then the other back-up pianist broke their arm, so I became the weekly accompanist. While I wasn't officially on staff, it felt nice to be needed beyond shuttling kids to and from their activities.

"Honk. Honk." I could see our oldest in the passenger seat pointing to his wrist as if wearing a watch. Something I often caught myself doing. Raising four kids on a tight budget was hard, but teaching them to follow the Lord and trust Him with big decisions was even harder, especially when we were scraping the bottom of the barrel.

I picked up my bag and tried not to look stressed as I stepped out onto the porch.

"Can we get a bite to eat?" my youngest asked when I slid into the driver's seat.

"Not today." I tried not to alarm our kids by sharing the news I had just heard. *God has a plan. I know He wouldn't just leave us stranded.*

I put the key in the ignition. The gas tank was half full, thankfully enough to get us through the rest of the week.

We drove down our short gravel driveway and stopped at the mailbox. *Hopefully it isn't just bills.*

I pulled the small stack into my lap and sorted through them briefly. One of the envelopes was from the church we had just started to attend. Why would they be writing to me?

I opened up the folded paper, and inside was a check written out to me for six weeks of playing as the church pianist. I hadn't filled anything out or applied for the job, but in the memo section of the check was the word STIPEND.

Tears flowed from my eyes. It was more than enough to help us get back on our feet while Todd continued to pursue a permanent job. It was more than enough to comfort me that we were in God's hands, no matter what our checking account balance was at the time. It was more than just the money—it was the abundance of peace that we really were right where the Lord wanted us to be.

"Mom," our son asked when he saw me wiping my face with the back of my hand. "Are you OK?"

"I'm more than just OK," I told him. "I actually have everything I need, and then some."

God's Mysterious Ways: Last-Minute Saves

Like children, sometimes we're running toward disaster without realizing it—or sometimes we see the disaster coming and don't know how to stop it. Sometimes it's not so much a disaster as an emotion like grief or despair that threatens to pull us into a pit. It's often at that edge that God meets us, pulls us away from the wrong path, and helps us realize that we're seen, we're loved, and we're strong enough to face whatever our next steps are.

- **Pray.** Whether or not prayer is already part of your morning routine, try taking a few seconds to stop and say a prayer like this: "God, whatever happens today, watch over me and help me make the right choices."

- **Seek.** When a decision or a moment of change comes upon you suddenly, it can be hard to take a step back to think. But when you see a difficult moment coming, don't forget to invite God in.

- **Act.** When you've received a blessing from God, do you have an opportunity to be a blessing to someone else, too?

- **Reflect.** Can you remember a time when you were at the brink of danger and God saved you? Or when you were in grief and God was there? Could there have been times He was carrying you and you didn't know it?

A Timely Coincidence

Marilyn Turk

The righteous choose their friends carefully, but the way of the wicked leads them astray.
—Proverbs 12:26 (NIV)

My oldest son didn't know what to do after high school. We lived in Georgia, but Jason wanted to attend the University of Florida, home of his favorite sports team, the Gators. Although Jason's grades were good enough to grant him a scholarship in his home state of Georgia, they weren't stellar enough to earn a scholarship at a Florida college.

Since I couldn't afford his out-of-state tuition, he decided to attend a small local Georgia college. However, the school just didn't live up to his dream college, so, discontented, he withdrew after one semester, and he went to work full time. Then my own circumstances changed, and I ended up moving to Florida.

After I'd lived there about a year, Jason asked to move in with me and go back to school at the local college near me to pull up his grades and then be able to enter the University of Florida as a resident and a junior. I agreed, and 2 years later, he achieved his goal, finally enrolling in the university of his dreams.

But by that time, Jason was several years older than his classmates. He didn't know anyone on campus and felt a little out of place. He found roommates for an off-campus apartment through the school, and I helped him move in and get a scooter so he could travel to and from the campus. I regularly prayed he'd make friends who'd be good influences, preferably Christian friends who might get him back into church, where he hadn't been for a while.

One day, shortly after the semester began, Jason texted me to tell me Tim Tebow, the star quarterback for the Gators, was in one of his classes. Jason's excitement permeated the text, and I was thrilled by his happiness about the "coincidence." Even more exciting was the day the teacher assigned students to study groups, placing Jason and Tim in the same group, along with two girls.

After their first meeting together, the girls were unable to attend the group again due to their other activities, so Jason and his hero Tim met by themselves, sometimes in a board room in the football stadium. As a result, they spent a lot of time together, and Jason got to know Tim as he demonstrated his Christian faith in his speech and actions. Jason witnessed how Tim treated others when adoring fans stopped him as they walked across campus, and Jason became the photographer when those fans requested pictures. Tim's accommodating behavior made a big impression on Jason, who would have otherwise been annoyed by such interruptions. But Tim never showed impatience or frustration, instead being cordial and friendly. Tim told Jason his own role model was the former University of Florida quarterback and Christian Danny Wuerffel, who had demonstrated the same behavior.

Jason called and texted me on a regular basis to tell me the latest news about his new friend Tim, like the time he gave Tim a ride on the back of his scooter to Tim's car. This mom's heart almost stopped as I visualized the sight of the tall star quarterback on the too-little seat of the motorbike.

When they graduated from college, Tim went on to become a well-known professional athlete, outspoken in his Christian beliefs. Although they lost contact with each other, Jason will never forget the influence Tim had on him during their time together. What a coincidence (not) that Jason attended college at the same time as his favorite football player. What a coincidence (not) that they ended up in a class, even a study group together. Who could have orchestrated the timing any more perfectly?

I couldn't have chosen a better friend or role model for my son. I couldn't have imagined a friendship like this for my son, but God could, in His fantastic way of answering prayers.

A Wink from God

Sara Etgen-Baker

You don't choose your family. They are God's gift to you, as you are to them.

—Desmond Tutu

I stood at the front door, wrapping my hand around the bronze doorknob, memorizing its patina, then twisted it until the weary front door opened. The seasons had taken their toll on it, baking it in summer and freezing it in winter. Now the door's once-brilliant blue paint was brittle and faded in the sunlight. I closed my eyes, remembering how often I'd passed through this door on my way to some new experience or another. I snapped the door shut behind me, enthusiastic about beginning the next chapter of my life.

I turned the key in my car's ignition and backed out of the driveway, bound for Indiana and my first post-college job. I cruised down the freeway, arriving hours later in Springfield, Missouri—the halfway point of my journey—to visit Granddad.

I pulled into his driveway and saw him sitting in his front porch swing. He waved, motioning me to join him. I sat down next to him, my eyes taking in the swing's familiar peeled white coat and rough wooden seat.

"What brings you my way?" Granddad asked.

"I'm going to Muncie, Indiana," I answered. The excitement of my new adventure mixed with the fear of the unknown, making my heart race. "I've taken a job at Ball State University!"

"Well now, that's great news! But," a slight frown creased his forehead, "why Muncie? Why so far from home?"

"I, uh . . . can't really explain it to you. For some inexplicable reason I was drawn to Muncie. Besides, you know Mom and Dad always raised me to be independent. Moving so far away lets me show them that I can make it on my own."

"Hmm. If you say so. You had dinner yet?"

"No sir."

"Well, then. Come inside. We'll eat. Leftovers OK with you?"

"Sure, Granddad, that'll be fine."

"Didn't your mother ever tell you?" he asked as we sat down for dinner.

"Tell me what?"

"Before settling in Missouri, my father migrated from Pennsylvania to Muncie. He worked in the gas fields for Ball Brothers Glass Manufacturing. Muncie was my boyhood home!" he exclaimed, his blue eyes twinkling. "So in a way, you're returning home."

"Really? I had no idea."

"Yes! What an amazing coincidence! My brother still lives in the house where I grew up. You must see it!" He reached for his telephone.

"Granddad, wait! No!" Uneasiness began stirring in my stomach. My goal had been to leave family behind and live independently, and here I was being pulled into a new circle of relatives. But I couldn't stop him.

"Hello, Claude. Bert here. Oh, me? Fine. You remember my granddaughter? She's moving to Muncie. And get this. She'll be working at Ball State. What? Sure. She'd love to meet you and the family. I'll give her your address."

Granddad hung up the telephone. "Here." He handed me a piece of paper with Claude's address scribbled on it. "Claude's eager to meet you."

"But Granddad." I stared at the piece of paper, "I don't know about that."

"Yes, I heard you say you wanted to be more independent," he asserted. "But your moving to Muncie is such a remarkable coincidence! You must be going there for a reason—but perhaps not for the reason you intended. You'll soon discover that reason."

"Maybe so, Granddad, but I don't know what the reason could be." I stuffed the piece of paper inside my jeans pocket and went to bed, wishing Granddad could understand and respect my need to assert my independence.

"Promise me you'll visit Claude," Granddad reiterated the next morning.

"All right, Granddad. I promise." The words stuck in my throat.

A few days after arriving in Muncie, I drove to Claude's house, wishing with all my heart that I hadn't promised Granddad I'd do so.

"Welcome!" Claude opened his front door, ushering me inside to an easy chair across from his fireplace. "I'm delighted to finally meet my great niece! I'm not much for words, but I've a lot to tell you about the family. I, uh . . . don't know where to begin," he said, his voice trailing off. He handed me a large, cumbersome volume with the words *Stainbrook/Steinbrook Family* embossed on the side binding. "This book will do a better job than I could; it tells our family story from the beginning. I'll leave you to it," Claude said, disappearing from the room.

The book was old and heavy, bound in green leather, and was cracked and dry with age. I eased back in the chair and

---

*"You must be going there for a reason—
but perhaps not for the reason you intended."*

---

propped my feet on a footstool, soaking in the warmth from his cheery fireplace and carefully fingering the gold lettering before opening the book. Words and images appeared and disappeared as I devoured the pages, immersed in the story of Jacob Steinbruchel, the first Stainbrook to come to the US, arriving in Philadelphia from Germany in 1747. He obtained his citizenship; bought land in Bucks County, Pennsylvania; and married. Before he was killed by Native Americans in 1757, he and his wife were blessed with three children— Maria, George, and Abraham—forever sealing their fate and the fortune of generations of Stainbrooks to follow as American citizens.

I paused and laid down the book, glancing at the richly carved mantel in front of me. It was filled with vintage family photos. I was attracted to a small oval portrait of a young woman. I stood up and stared at her photograph. Her gaze, undimmed by time, met mine, and I immediately felt a deep, enigmatic connection to her. The smile on her face comforted me, and I sensed her love for me—a love as real as if she were in the room with me.

"You have her strong cheek bones," Claude observed as he reentered the room. "The resemblance is uncanny."

"Who is she?"

"You never knew her; she's your great-grandmother, Martha Elizabeth Burrus-Stainbrook. She was your age when this photo was taken."

But Claude was wrong. I'd known her face forever. I'd seen it long before I knew this photograph existed, for Martha's features and countenance were the same ones I'd seen on my mother's face.

At that moment, my perspective shifted. I recognized that God had orchestrated my move to Muncie but, as Granddad suggested, not for the reason I intended. Rather than distancing myself from family, I was in Muncie to learn more about my heritage and to bond with family in a much broader sense.

For 3 years I lived and worked in Muncie, spending a great deal of time with Claude and a host of other Stainbrooks. I'm grateful for my time with them, for my life was richer for it. Granddad was right. That mysterious urge I had to move to Muncie wasn't just an amazing coincidence, it was guidance from God. I've come to appreciate such interventions, realizing that God speaks directly to each of us and guides us to His purpose—sometimes in the most unexpected ways.

A Ride Home

John Seither, as told to Marci Seither

Search me, God, and know my heart; test me and know my anxious thoughts.

—Psalm 139:23 (NIV)

The economy was taking a drastic turn. House foundations were abandoned with just the pipes coming out of the slabs, and the people I had worked for started looking for other jobs. I was left wondering how I was going to provide for my young family. We had some equity in our home, but the housing market had also screeched to a halt. Even if we wanted to move, it was not going to be easy. I looked into any job opportunity I could think of and called around to companies I had worked with when I was running our concrete pumping business. No one was hiring. I looked at all my options, but the economic future didn't look bright, at least not where we were living.

My own dad was not someone I could count on as reliable. His constant drinking and broken promises made trusting the Lord something that didn't come naturally for me. If I couldn't trust my own dad to take care of his family, could I trust the Lord as a father figure with my family and our future?

Now, facing the realities of day-to-day life with little income, I grew a garden, built a small chicken coop, and put up a clothes line so we could cut our expenses. But it still was a struggle, and with every passing month I felt my anxiety rise despite my wife's optimism that the Lord would not abandon us.

One afternoon I received a call from a friend I had known when I was in the military service years earlier. It was a welcome surprise. We chatted for at least an hour, catching up on what we were doing and how the Lord was working in our lives. It wasn't until I hung up with Ken that I realized the topic of economic downturn hadn't been part of our discussion. Another welcome surprise.

"Maybe we need to think outside of California?" my wife suggested. I booked a ticket to visit my friend in Fergus Falls, Minnesota and spent a week checking out the quaint town, churches, and possible houses. It seemed like I had just stepped onto the set of *The Andy Griffith Show* and walked the streets of Mayberry. When I came home, we put our house on the market. The previous month over seven hundred homes in our county were listed for sale, and only seven had sold. It was a long shot, but if the Lord was going to open the door for us to leave, we would need to sell our home. If we didn't sell it, I would take that as a closed door.

Before long, someone inquired about our house and bought it. We put an offer in on an old farmhouse I had seen when I had been in Minnesota. It had several acres where our kids could run around, a chicken coop, and an old barn.

Marci started packing up our belongings while I was tying up loose ends with our business. But, even with selling as much as we could, it seemed like we were barely going to make our savings last long enough to cover all our bills and moving expenses. Not only were we running out of time and money, I was running out of energy. I had been faithfully praying and fasting. *Please Lord, show us the right thing to do. Help me make the decisions that would be best for my family.*

One of the last things I needed to do was finish the concrete pumping job I was on and deliver the big machine to the person who was purchasing it. Another huge prayer had been

---

"Lord," I half-heartedly prayed. "It would save me quite a bit if you could arrange for a ride..."

---

to find a buyer for my equipment as well as one for our home. We ended up with a buyer for both, but instead of collecting the money I had hoped we would have in hand for our move, we ended up carrying papers—we would be getting payments and taking the risk of someone defaulting on the deal. Not an ideal situation, but one I was going to have to trust to the Lord's care.

"I guess You provided," I prayed one day. "I just wish I had been a bit more specific on the terms."

As I bounced along on the narrow back road to deliver the truck to the buyer, I felt the weight of our move pressing down on me and looked at the gas gauge. If I drove the pump all the way home and then dropped it off, it was going to be an extra 50 miles and require a stop to fuel up. More money. I could almost hear it draining from our family banking account into the gas tank.

"Lord," I half-heartedly prayed. "It would save me quite a bit if you could arrange for a ride instead of driving this big machine all the way home." I felt guilty for being so petty in my request. God wasn't my carpool coordinator.

I glanced in my rearview mirror.

Instead of an empty, tree-lined road, there was a large white passenger van behind me. Not just any van. This one belonged to our friends, who happened to live down the street from us in our small mountain town.

I got close to a turnoff and waved our friend over. He quickly agreed to give me a ride back home so I could take the pump directly to the buyer the next day.

"What are the chances I would be right behind you? I hardly ever take this road!" our friend said after we got to a place I could park the big concrete pump for the evening. I was greeted with the cheerful sounds of their kids in the seats behind me. "Seriously, I think I've only taken this road a few times a year."

That "accidental" meeting had saved me some much-needed money. But of much greater value was knowing that if the Lord had opened the door for the sale of our home and answered my halfhearted prayer for a ride, I could trust Him with moving my family halfway across the country. My Father had let me know He would always be there.

Now That I'm Sixty-Four

Linda Marie Cumbie

The beauty of a woman is not in a facial mode but the true beauty in a woman is reflected in her soul. It is the caring that she lovingly gives the passion that she shows. The beauty of a woman grows with the passing of years.

—Audrey Hepburn

I have lived my whole life with a scar that starts at the corner of my mouth and goes up my cheek, a result of removing a tumor that had been in my mouth at birth. By some miracle, when I smile the scar disappears into the folds of my cheek and becomes invisible. Still, when I was younger there were times that someone said something unkind about the scar, and it made me insecure about my looks. Now, looking back at old pictures, I realize that I was physically beautiful.

As my sixty-fourth birthday approached, I was going through a hard time. Over the years my scar has become more prominent, and I have gained a significant amount of weight. I was feeling unattractive. So, the month before my birthday, I had a request for God: "I know this is superficial, but still, could You let me be beautiful one more time in my life before I die? I know You can do miracles." I felt guilty asking for this when there are so many problems in the world, but it was my sincere wish.

A week later I was in a group of people and one of the ladies said, "You have the most beautiful eyes," I was surprised and replied, "People used to say that when I was younger, but it's been a long time. Thank you."

The following week I was in a convenience store that I had been to several times before. Out of the blue the young man behind the counter asked, "How old are you?" Although it was before my birthday, I said, "Sixty-four." He then said, "You're beautiful." It was such a strange thing to say in that moment—coming on the heels of my prayer—and I could tell he wasn't trying to pick me up. Again, I deflected the compliment and hurried out of the store.

The next day I went to a Bible study and was asked to read a portion of some affirmations that we were given. This is what I read:

I am God's beloved child in whom He is well pleased. I am fearfully and wonderfully made, beautiful beyond measure. The power of God guards my thoughts, the Word of God guides my steps, and the favor of God rests on me.

I kept on looking in the mirror, hoping for some sign of the beauty others said they were seeing, but I didn't look any different to myself.

On the day of my sixty-fourth birthday, I was invited to a garden tea party. I should have been excited about it, but I had nothing to wear, and when I shopped, I could not find anything in my size. I was sad because, superficial as it was, I knew there would be a lot of pictures taken, and I hated having my picture taken.

The actual day of my birthday came, and that morning I read a devotional by Gail Goleas, editor of the devotional magazine *Living in Faith*. In the devotional, she talked about a woman, Victoria, who aided the Allies in WWII. Because she would not betray them, the Nazis threw a vial of acid on her face. Gale wrote of how Victoria bore those scars with grace. The last line of the devotion read: "It wasn't the scars one noticed, but God's goodness in her eyes."

I had not been through the things this woman, Victoria, had been through, but her message spoke to me of something far greater than outer beauty—an inner beauty that will shine through to our outer countenance. Reading it when I did, the morning of my birthday, was the best present I could have gotten. Instead of fretting over how I looked, I went to the party with a grateful heart, thankful for friends and such a nice way to spend the day.

The tea party was a visual paradise. It was in the back of a beautiful nineteenth-century home. The grass was lush and green, and the area was surrounded by live oak trees and flowers of many colors. Each table was set with unique and precious tableware. The person in charge of each table told the story of the porcelain tableware, how it came into their family and about the tradition of holding these teas. My friends had remembered my birthday and had well wishes and presents.

At the end of the day, they gave out door prizes. I won one of the prizes, and it was in a bag that said, "Be bold and beautiful!"

"Thank You," I said to God. "I get the message."

Little Prayer, Big Blessing

Loraine McElhaney

Before they call, I will answer; while they are still speaking, I will hear.

—Isaiah 65:24 (NIV)

It had been several years since I shared my love of jewelry crafting with a delightful group of women, residents in a recovery program. I supplied the materials and patterns while they brought enthusiasm and laughter. I was blessed. It brought me joy to see those going through difficult circumstances having fun.

One of the ladies made a complicated bracelet with small beads and pearls. When she cut the thread too close to the knot, it broke near the closure. Because our class was ending for that day, I told her I would fix it and bring it back. The next few weeks were chaotic. Most of the residents were graduating and moving on to the next steps in their lives. I never saw her again.

Recently, I was clearing the clutter from my craft room when I came across a sandwich bag containing her bracelet. I said a little prayer: *Lord, I can't even remember her name.*

I would like to give the bracelet back to her, but I have no way of contacting her.

The prayer was that brief and ended with a sigh on my part. What were the chances of my finding her? My contacts at the program had gone to other jobs. To me, the task of locating her seemed daunting. I promptly put that short request out of my mind. Little did I realize that God heard and was working to answer my small petition.

A few weeks later I called a pet boarding and day-care facility with a request to bring our dog, Molly, there. When my husband Barry and I adopted her from the animal shelter, we did not initially realize our 33-pound, mostly white, mixed-breed dog was deaf. Only when she did not respond to sudden, loud noises did it occur to us she was hearing impaired. Molly also has a serious attachment problem. She will nap with part of her body on a person's foot if one is sitting in a chair. While we are home, she shadows either my husband or me. We cannot leave her to roam the house for a short while because she will counter surf to look for any food particles available. I have seen her leap, as though she was spring loaded, onto the kitchen table.

I tell her, "Molly, you need to grow up to be a big girl." Being deaf, she has no clue. We needed a place to take her for a few hours occasionally so we could have some respite time without worries.

I made arrangements for an interview at a pet care center. We would leave Molly for 3 to 4 hours for them to see how she interacted with the other dogs. We brought the papers to show her shots were current and left to go out to breakfast. I was relieved we did not receive a call to come and retrieve our dog. When we returned, we were given a tour of the facility and were able to view Molly along with the other dogs. My fears were alleviated when I saw our beloved pet was not curled up in a corner. Maybe this was a step in the right direction.

When we walked back to the front, a lady at the reception counter, who was not present when we first came in, asked me, "Did you teach beading at a recovery program?"

When I replied, "Yes," I realized that this was the one whose bracelet I had prayed over just a few weeks prior. I asked, "Remind me of your name."

"Rachel," she replied. She shared that she worked only 2 days per week. Wednesday was one of those days when we took Molly into that kennel. Then she told me she groomed dogs and was not always at the front desk. Time did not permit me to tell her the entire story.

I look at this series of events as a personal miracle. If I had taken Molly to doggy daycare any other day, I would have missed an opportunity to be blessed again.

It was a few weeks before I could return the bracelet to Rachel. I wanted to make certain she knew about my short petition and what transpired over the weeks, so when I gave her the bracelet, I included a short note about my prayer. Later, Rachel sent me a thank-you email. She shared that she was at a time in her life where God seemed distant. This impacted her in a positive way.

Little miracles can have a ripple effect. Not only did I have an amazing experience of God at work, but I can tuck away the memory for the future. If, like Rachel, I'm ever in a place where I wonder if God is present, I have this reminder that He hears our prayers and responds in ways beyond our imagination.

God's Mysterious Ways: He Remembers

Sometimes we pray for something we want and it doesn't come. We don't have God's wisdom; sometimes the things that we want aren't the best for us or for others. But sometimes the answer isn't "no," it's just "not right now," or "wait and see what I've got in store for you!"

Sometimes we just forget—we forget something small, like a task we meant to do, or something big, like the fact that we're beautiful and loved by God. But God always remembers.

- **Pray.** Is there something you need God's help doing? Or do you have that nagging feeling you've forgotten something? Here's a prayer you can use: "God, help me to remember something important today."

- **Seek.** Pay attention to little signs. Did you come across a reminder of something that you need to finish? Or something you'd forgotten?

- **Act.** Choose something—a small item or token—to remind you that God watches over you, and carry it with you today. Or, if you already have one, bring a different one today, one that will stand out in your mind.

- **Reflect.** Have your prayers ever been answered with "wait"? How long did it take you to realize that was the answer? Looking back, do you see a message in the way things worked out?

A Girl Named Beth

Kristen West

I knew when I met you an adventure was going to happen.
—Winnie the Pooh

Have you ever had those chance meetings that, as you look back on them, were clearly divine appointments that changed your life forever?

For me, it was when I met Beth.

It was the beginning of my sophomore year in high school. I had just started internally grappling with questions like, *Why am I here? Why was I made? What's my purpose? What happens when I die?* I was raised in a religious environment. Went to church weekly. Attended youth group. Yet the answers to those all-important questions remained elusive.

I tried out for the girls' basketball team and made it. Arriving at our first practice of the season, I noticed Beth. Rumor was she had recently moved into our little Michigan community from Minnesota. She was unobtrusive, quiet, meek, and an outstanding basketball player.

From a distance, I liked her immediately. I didn't have any real close friends. I got along with virtually everyone, but I didn't have a tight-knit circle that I fit into. Beth just seemed like the type of person I would click with, and as it turned out, I was right.

Over the course of our basketball season together, we became fast friends. We had a similar sense of humor, like-minded interests, and both of us loved Kentucky Fried Chicken nuggets (an important ingredient in our budding teenage friendship).

Beth knew Jesus. Unlike me, however, she actually had a personal relationship with Him. I had no idea what that was. To me, going to church was what made you a Christian. And yet, over the course of our young friendship, Beth didn't push her theology on me. She didn't condemn me for my religious blindness. She didn't try to manipulate or pressure me into a "come to Jesus" decision that I wasn't ready to make. She simply lived out her faith in front of me. It was authentic, consistent, and kind. It often convicted me, although I wasn't willing to acknowledge that yet. Beth met me where I was and loved me in spite of my selfishness.

She walked a victorious life—one of peace, joy, and grace. The more I witnessed it, the more I wanted it for myself.

A few months elapsed. My internal grapplings had morphed into deep angst. I would cry myself to sleep nightly as I struggled with eternal questions: What would happen when I die? Why did I exist? What meaning did my life have? Looking back, I realize that it was my hunger to feel seen, valued, known, and loved in all areas of my life, especially within my family. I felt a need for a deeper love—God's love. But no one was aware of my inner turmoil. I intentionally kept it hidden.

The summer before my senior year of high school, Beth and I had gone to the local A&W to grab a burger and a root beer. I was consumed with worry about life. I was at the breaking point with those nagging, internal questions;

I longed for answers. Fear and frustrations about my future had mounted so much in my young heart and mind that, try as I may, I couldn't stop them from seeping into our conversation that day.

"Do you have a Bible?" Beth asked, seeing my troubled state.

"Yeah," I replied.

> *She simply lived out her faith in front of me.*
> *It was authentic, consistent, and kind.*

"When you get home today, look up Philippians 4:6 and 7," she said.

"OK," I responded dismally.

Beth had no idea how excited that simple suggestion had made me, even though outwardly I had projected a blasé front. I wanted to run home and find my Precious Moments Bible so I could see what those verses said, desperate for answers that could give me the kind of peace that Beth had.

The moment I got home, I made a beeline for my room. Closing the door, I began rummaging to find where that Bible was buried.

I found it and looked up Philippians 4:6 and 7. "Don't worry about anything, but in everything, through prayer and petition with thanksgiving, present your requests to God. And the peace of God, which surpasses all understanding, will guard your hearts and minds in Christ Jesus" (CSB).

I never recalled seeing those verses before. My mind wrestled with that phrase "don't worry about anything." *How is that even humanly possible?* I wondered. In that moment, I couldn't imagine that level of freedom. I was confused, yet hopeful. Perplexed, yet interested.

A few short weeks later, I was alone in my bedroom when I fell to my knees. I had been wrestling with the idea of giving my life to Christ. Over the previous week, I'd created a list of the things that wouldn't be compatible with living as a Christian, such as the secular music I enjoyed, and my non-Christian boyfriend. Sitting in my bedroom that night, staring at the list, I knew in my heart that Jesus's love was greater than anything I might lose by giving Him my heart. Tears poured from my eyes as I surrendered my life to God.

When I got up, I knew I was different. Jesus was my Lord. He had made me new. He had taken my worries and given me His promised peace. In that space, He began to help me understand the answers to those eternal questions. What joy!

My thoughts immediately went to Beth. I needed to tell her what had happened so she could share this life-changing moment with me!

Beth and I spent the rest of that very special day together on the shores of Lake Superior, watching the sun set while I riddled her with questions about God, what my next steps were now as a new Christian, and where was the best place to begin reading my Bible.

Our meeting was no coincidence. God knew what—and who—I needed during that very turbulent time in my life. He perfectly arranged for a young girl to move into my town, my high school, and my life in order to set me on a trajectory toward Him and the future I would live for His glory!

A Mother's Day Connection

Glenda Ferguson

My Father's way may twist and turn,
My heart may throb and ache;
But in my soul I'm glad to know
He maketh no mistake.

—"He Maketh No Mistake" by A. M. Overton

I lied to my mom. Not to her face. She would have detected my deception. Over the phone, I explained I wouldn't be traveling from Indiana to Missouri for Mother's Day. My hectic schedule consisted of commuting an hour one way, working at Indiana University, attending night classes, and studying. All those reasons sounded believable and exhausting. The real reason? I was broke.

After only a few months, I regretted my impulsive decision to move to another state for graduate school.

Back in Missouri, I taught at a private elementary school within walking distance of my apartment. I was only 20 minutes away from Mom's house. Unexpectedly, the school eliminated my teaching job. Pursuing my master's degree seemed like a grand adventure. I chose Indiana

University when the education department offered me a partial scholarship.

But expenses were more than I had anticipated. Instead of living near campus, I settled south in a cheaper apartment. Keeping my fuel tank full cut into my budget for groceries, utilities, and tuition. With Mom, I could open up about my daily struggles regarding my studies, but not about my embarrassing financial situation. My caring mom would have sent money. I was too proud to ask.

God, would Mom forgive me if she knew?

Mom said, "I told everyone you would be busy. Before you know it, you'll be home for summer barbecues."

Just the mention of barbecue made my mouth water. The Mother's Day menu included chicken on the grill, homemade potato salad, and smoky baked beans. Mom mixed up a sky-high angel-food cake with pink frosting. My affordable meal would be a box of mac 'n cheese.

Mom ended our usual Saturday morning call with her pet name for me, "Love you, my sweet angel."

The tears flowed. Mom and I were best friends. We enjoyed the outdoors in every season—fishing in the creek, walking on country roads admiring the fall colors, slogging through snow, and listening to the spring songbirds.

Remembering those good times brought Mother's Day cards to mind. Mom saved every greeting card from me, along with my poems and drawings embellished with glitter. She particularly liked the nature scene cards. Every year, choosing the perfect one had been an important and lengthy process at our local drugstore. I scrutinized the image on the front, and I was just as selective about the inside message.

Until this year. Not wanting to think about finances, or the fact that I wouldn't be home for her special day, I'd put off looking for a card. Now, the day before, I still hadn't purchased one.

On impulse, I grabbed my car keys and spare change. One of the downtown stores, only a few minutes away, stocked an extensive card collection.

I circled the town square twice, searching for a parking spot. Visiting this popular store on a busy Saturday was a foolish decision. Even more foolish? Wasting precious fuel.

The town's charming drugstore had become my favorite. I knew the card selection would be on the right as I stepped inside. I veered to the left to catch a whiff of the scented candles. Wild rose reminded me of the bushes at Mom's house. I smiled as I passed by the shelf of angel figurines, then proceeded to the display.

Only a few Mother's Day cards were left. *Serves me right for delaying.*

As I looked over the display, a glossy photo caught my eye—pink roses in full bloom and flowing script reading "You're a Wonderful Mother." I slowly traced the smooth petals and the bumpy glittery edges. The inside expressed my sentiment exactly—it spoke about taking every chance to tell Mom how loved she was.

I just knew. *This is the one.*

As I walked to the counter, I tucked the card and matching pink envelope under my arm and tallied my change. Only one customer was in front of me. She was about Mom's age and height but with dark hair. She leisurely spun the nearby revolving rack of Indiana postcards. I overheard her remark to the clerk that she was purchasing a few to take back to Missouri.

I interrupted them. "Are you from Missouri? I grew up there."

The lady said, "Yes, I live there now. I was born in northern Indiana. That's where I've been visiting." Her name was Wanda, from a Missouri town just about a hundred miles from Mom. She mentioned her son's alma mater, College of the Ozarks.

"I graduated from there too," I said and told her the year. I remembered her son. We attended some of the same classes.

Every year, choosing the perfect Mother's Day card had been an important and lengthy process. I scrutinized the image on the front, and I was just as selective about the inside message.

I recalled those first months at college, missing home and questioning God about my career plans. I was occupied with several classes, studying, and a campus job. Similar to my circumstances now. Mom's weekly letters kept me going, especially her humorous drawings or newspaper clippings. I now treasure those college memories.

After paying, we continued our conversation outside. I told Wanda about my recent plans. Her soothing voice was so kind and pleasant. This was almost like talking to Mom.

She said, "I saw you buying a Mother's Day card decorated with roses. That's my favorite type of card too. You must miss your mom."

I was getting emotional just attempting to respond. "I guess that's why I started talking to you, because of your Missouri connection. This is the first time in 5 years that I'm not going to be there for Mother's Day." I couldn't look her in the eye.

Wanda said, "Your mom must be proud of your success in your new life. You will have a lot to talk about when you do see her. God's timing is always perfect."

We decided to keep in touch and exchanged addresses. I thanked her for the encouragement.

As we were about to part, Wanda said, "Do you hear the songbirds?"

Actually, all I heard was the traffic noise.

"Just listen. Those birds are harbingers of spring," she said. "There are good things to come!"

After returning to my apartment, I thought about what Wanda said. I even looked up "harbinger"—a messenger that announces or signals the approach of an event. Wanda was right. She and I met, not by chance, but by God's plan. Inside Mom's card, I wrote all about my encounter and included what Wanda had said about there being other chances for us to be together.

I could hear the songbirds outside my window. They had been signaling me all along. God would continue guiding me, just as He guided Wanda to that store at just the right moment to comfort me, and I knew that when the time was right He would bring me home.

God Is Always Listening

Jesse Neve

You will pray to Him, and He will hear you.
—Job 22:27 (NASB)

Glass half full. Looking on the bright side. Maybe even a bit Pollyanna-ish. Ever since I was young, I looked at situations differently than most people. The silver linings always shone brightly to me.

So when my parents divorced when I was five and my mom remarried, I thought I was *so lucky* to have *three* parents, when most people only had *two*! I had my house with my cool purple room and all of my cats with my mom, my stepdad, and my new baby sister, and then I also got to spend weekends with Papa at his house. I thought I had the best of both worlds.

Papa and I had wonderful weekend adventures together, but growing up, I always prayed for two things.

The first was that my two separate families could get together and celebrate special occasions together. My mom and Papa didn't ever really talk to each other. They weren't angry at each other, just not friends. Birthdays and Christmases were awesome getting to celebrate twice, but I always thought, *Wouldn't it be neat if we could all be at the same party?*

Second, when I was in elementary school, I would imagine that Papa was at the window of my classroom, watching the great job I was doing at being a student and following the rules. I prayed that one day Papa would appear and watch me performing my normal daily tasks.

Fast forward twenty-some years. I was married and had four children between the ages of one and seven. Papa had been diagnosed with early onset Alzheimer's disease at the shockingly young age of 52, and he had moved in with our family when he was no longer able to care for himself.

"Mom, how are we going to do this?" I said over the phone after we had invited Papa to live with us. "Papa is going to be here all the time, but we still want you to come and visit. We don't want it to be weird."

"Not a problem," Mom replied confidently. "We are just going to get over our past and all be friends." I was so relieved that my mom had decided to be positive and help the situation.

The first birthday dinner arrived. I found myself seated next to my sister—the daughter of my mom and my stepdad—and I looked around the table at Mom, Papa, my stepdad Doug, and my whole little crowd. Here we were, all celebrating together.

I leaned over and whispered to my sister, "Can you believe this? Weirdest thing ever." We watched as my three parents chatted and joked with each other.

"Yes, but nobody else seems to think so," she replied, "It's so amazing."

Shortly after that first big birthday dinner together, in the middle of a day, when my kids were at school, I decided it was time to scrub the kitchen floor, since there was nobody around to dart across the floor and mess it up. I put chairs in front of the entrances to the room and started in with my bucket and rag, on my hands and knees.

Moments later, I had the unnerving feeling of being watched. I turned my head and found Papa standing near the blockade, just watching me.

"What 'cha doin'?" I asked, wondering if he needed something in the kitchen.

"Oh, just watching you work. The floor looks good," he replied with a smile and nod of approval.

And watch me he did. He stood there for the entire time it took me to wash the floor. Not until the very end, when I was rinsing out my bucket, did I understand that this is what I had been praying about years earlier—for Papa to just come and watch me do my work.

We spent the next 10 years of holidays and birthdays celebrating together, with Mom and Doug treating Papa as another member of the family. And having Papa living with me, sharing our everyday lives, brought us closer than ever.

The answers to my prayers weren't exactly what I had in mind when I was a child. Nobody wants their loved ones to be stricken with such a horrible disease. But God is always listening, and He knows how to turn even the worst circumstances into a blessing. He just answers our prayers on His own terms, in His own time.

The Path That Led Me to My Perfect Pet

Sarah Cole

I will heal them; I will guide them and restore comfort to Israel's mourners.

—Isaiah 57:18 (NIV)

My love affair with dogs began when my parents adopted our wiener dog, Sherman. I loved watching him chase his tail and bark at his reflection on the patio door. When I got bigger, we wrestled on the living room carpet, and I giggled when he licked me all over my face. For years we were inseparable, but at 15, he suffered from severe back pain, so my parents had him put to sleep.

Many dogs have come and gone since, but after my cocker spaniel died, I couldn't handle another loss, so I started fostering. It had been a few months since my last foster dog, and I'd just signed up to foster a new one when Lydia, a friend at my church, asked me to adopt her 15-year-old shih tzu-poodle mix. Lydia was being treated for cancer, and between that and caring for her husband, Jim, who had dementia, Zoe was too much to handle. Lydia knew I was on a tight budget and offered to cover Zoe's expenses. "This is a God thing!" I said to myself. Even though I had wanted a younger dog, here was someone with a dog who needed a home at just the time when I was ready to adopt.

On her good days, Lydia attended my church. At 85, Lydia sported purple hair that said she wasn't afraid to be noticed. It symbolized her zest for life and unwavering courage. Despite her illness, she refused to be a victim and never complained— a role model for all of us.

Although it took my adopted dog a while to warm up to me, eventually she welcomed me home with her toothless smile and demanded to be on my lap at every opportunity.

On adoption day, Lydia waited in the lobby of her apartment building to welcome me with a big smile. "Hi, Sarah! It's good to see you. Thank you so much for adopting Zoe!" she said.

As we walked down the hallway, I asked her how she felt. "I had a blood transfusion yesterday and am much better," she said.

We sat in the living room of her one-bedroom apartment while Zoe napped, oblivious to her fate. Lydia told me that life was different now that Jim was in the nursing home.

"How are you holding up?" I asked.

"It's depressing here by myself," she admitted. The chemotherapy made her so weak that she often crawled on the floor.

"There are days I just can't function," she said with a tear. "But I'm so relieved I don't have to put Zoe down," she said.

"It's the least I can do!" I replied.

We discussed Zoe's diet and quirky habits, like barking at her reflection on the patio door. She was incontinent and wore diapers; the first thing that came to mind was my poor carpeting! After she woke up, I patted her head, and she took a few steps backward and growled. *At her age, she has a right to be cranky,* I thought.

After Lydia and I said goodbye, I gathered Zoe's belongings and walked her to the car in the frigid air. While I cleaned off the windshield, she sat on the passenger seat shivering, so I covered her with Lydia's purple afghan.

Zoe stared quizzically at me beneath her long, matted hair. She hadn't seen a vet or a groomer for over a year, and her missing teeth and bad breath repelled me. But Zoe was about to get a makeover.

While I was gone the next day, she must have thought the upstairs carpeting was a toilet. When I scolded her, God told me, *Zoe's a gift, but you treat her like a liability.* That sure shut me up!

Over the coming months, I began to see Zoe's good points. She was laid back, friendly without demanding constant attention, and not held back by her physical limitations. Although it took her a while to warm up to me, eventually she welcomed me home with her toothless smile and demanded to be on my lap at every opportunity. We became best buddies. God sure knew what He was doing!

Lydia and I never lost touch, and she was grateful for my weekly progress reports and photos of Zoe. Then, after a routine colonoscopy, she received a second cancer diagnosis. Devastated and alone, she moved to the nursing home across the hall from Jim. My heart broke for her, but I was happy God had reunited them.

After Lydia got settled, Zoe and I stopped by for a visit. Jim sat in his wheelchair, smiling, while Lydia rested in her recliner beside her knitting basket. Jim understood little, but he remembered Zoe was his best friend and smiled while she sat on his lap. Reuniting them blessed me.

When Lydia stopped answering my texts, I knew it wasn't good, so I left her a voicemail encouraging her that she could have hope because Jesus eagerly waited to welcome her.

Lydia's passing a week later saddened me, but my heart rejoiced at her reunion with Jesus. When we gathered at her memorial, tears flowed as we remembered her sweet spirit, unrelenting courage, and joyful attitude.

In a short time, I bonded with two good friends. Lydia taught me how to be brave and trust God. Zoe taught me to be resilient and—through her example of learning to trust a stranger after having spent almost her entire life with someone else—encouraged me to give others a chance, too. God's greatest gifts come in unexpected packages. He knows what we need better than we do. That's why He led Lydia to ask me about adopting Zoe at just the moment in my life when I was ready to adopt her.

Ultimately, I don't know if I rescued Zoe or if she rescued me, but I'm grateful God loved us enough to make it possible.

No Better Name for a New Friend

Beth Gormong

Greet the friends there by name.
—3 John 1:15 (NIV)

For nearly 28 years, my husband, Jeff, and I had called a secluded rural county our home, but my new job required a move to the city. We signed a one-year lease for a small apartment right off one of the busiest streets. Suddenly, we had hundreds of neighbors, but they were all strangers. Jeff's job meant he worked from home while I went to the office every weekday. He knew no one and went nowhere except for church on Sundays. He was lonely.

A few Sundays after we moved into our apartment complex, we climbed down the stairs and walked to our car. As we prepared to pull out of our parking spot, a car passed us, stopped, and made a U-turn. The window rolled down to reveal a man about our age. "I saw your Bible. Are you heading to church?" he asked.

When we nodded yes, he continued. "I could tell you were good people. My mom just died. I've been here from out of town helping my dad with the funeral and such. Would you be willing to stop in and check on him periodically after I leave Tuesday? He lives in the first apartment in that building." He pointed down the road to a distant unit. "His name is Dave Duncan. My mom was Shirley."

"We're sorry for your loss," we told this stranger, and promised to visit his father.

As Jeff rolled his car window up and drove the car out of the complex, we discussed how odd, yet encouraging, the interaction had been. To be seen as a safe couple, as people who this grieving son felt comfortable approaching gave us joy.

"And isn't it amazing that Dave and Shirley have the same names as another couple we know?" I marveled. "Perhaps that means Dave Duncan will be our first friend in the apartment complex."

"Let's make a meal and get a card," Jeff suggested.

"Should we take a meal? We are complete strangers to Dave," I worried.

In the end, Jeff came up with a solution. "What if we buy a sympathy card and put a gift certificate in it from the local restaurant across that street that everyone keeps telling us about? Then we can take it to Dave on our way home."

When we dropped the gift off, Dave wasn't there, so we left it on his porch with our names, phone numbers, and apartment number included with our signatures.

The next day Dave sent a thank-you text. On Saturday, Jeff came back from the local farmers market with a dozen ears of corn—some for us and some for Dave. He delivered the corn and chatted with Dave for a while.

While I was out of town for a week, Jeff and Dave visited, and a sweet friendship began, one of mutual small gifts of kindness. Dave reciprocated the sweet corn gift when he bought more than he could eat. Then he and his visiting daughter brought by some pumpkin bread when Jeff was recovering from an illness. Dave stopped by occasionally, sent Jeff texts, and called sporadically.

Soon our year-long lease was over, and we moved into our new home. Jeff let Dave know we were moving down the street. Dave let us know he was also moving away to be nearer to his children.

Through a chance meeting—a glimpse of a Bible that let someone know we were people of faith—God gave Jeff a friend when he needed it most, in a new town, and gave Dave a friend during his grieving process.

We thought that one seeming coincidence—a new friend with the same name as people we'd known before—would be enough, but God had more in store for us. In the driveway of our new home, our next-door neighbor introduced himself. "I'm Mark, and this is my beagle, Charlie."

As soon as we were in the house, I turned toward my husband in amazement. "Jeff! Those are the exact names of your two best college friends. And Charlie is a beagle just like our beloved dog, Max!"

God's voice was very clear once again. And to this very day He keeps letting us know he's providing friends in the sweetest ways.

An Amazing Gift

Isabella Parker

The greatest gift of life is friendship, and I have received it.
—Hubert H. Humphrey

My friend Marian was excellently eccentric. She marched to the beat of her own drum and let her inner weirdness dictate life decisions. She put her own spin on everything she did, and that included gift-giving. Marian gave gifts that had meaning. If she saw something that reminded her of a particular moment she had experienced with you, then that's what she gifted to you. It didn't have to be new, clean, complete, beautiful, or even wrapped. She looked beyond flashy consumer packaging and big price tags. One year for my birthday, she gave me a large bottle of Ivory dish soap that she had gotten free at a local food bank because I had told her once that the smell of Ivory dish soap reminded me of my grandmother and my childhood. And so when she saw that bottle of Ivory, she said she knew it was meant for me. If you were a friend of Marian's, you really came to expect and cherish these incredibly odd gifts.

The Christmas of 2020 was very difficult for me. In a period of six months, I had lost my grandmother, my favorite uncle, and my fiancé to Covid. Because of my job working with intellectually disabled adults in the "at risk" category, I had to be quarantined at home long after the restrictions were lifted for others.

Meanwhile, Marian spent her time taking care of the sick. She made chicken soup and delivered toilet paper to shut-ins. While the rest of us were hoarding food, she was out looking for food with which to bless others.

On Christmas Eve, there was a knock at my front door, and when I opened it, there stood Marian with a smile that illuminated her entire face. "Merry Christmas!" she exclaimed as she handed me a gift bag with "Happy Birthday" written across the front that had been used more than a few times.

"Oh, Marian, I'm sorry I didn't get you anything. I didn't realize we were doing a gift exchange." The pandemic had changed the rules and blurred the lines of everything that year, including the holidays.

"No, no, I wasn't expecting anything," she assured me with a wave of the hand. "I was at a clothing closet looking for a winter coat for myself and I came across this. I just *knew* it was meant for you!" She started giggling like a schoolgirl as I looked into the bag.

Inside that worn and wrinkled bag was a pair of bright-green socks with the word "Amazing" printed on the bottom and a bottle of Jergens lotion. I stood there staring at those ugly green socks. I was shocked into silence.

"Isn't God good?" she said.

Yes, in fact, God is good. Very good.

You see, my name is Isabella Grace, and almost everyone just calls me Grace. My fiancé had always called me "Amazing." It was his term of endearment for me. Marian had loved that he called me that. She always said it matched me. I never felt particularly amazing, but I have to admit, it made me feel very special when he called me by that nickname. He passed away so unexpectedly and without a chance to say goodbye. I had been devastated by the loss and hadn't taken the time to process or heal.

There I stood, holding a pair of socks with the word *Amazing* across the bottom. It was a surreal moment. I felt like God was reminding me that I was amazing and that He was still with me.

"I just knew it was meant for you!" She started giggling like a schoolgirl as I looked into the bag.

Marian said the lotion was to bring back memories of my grandmother, who I had also lost to the virus. She told me that anytime I needed to be near my grandmother, to just smell the Jergens. "Remember, Grace, that you are amazing and very loved."

A couple of used gifts in a tattered bag. The bottle of lotion was half empty and had goop in the top from previous uses. The socks had holes in the toes. But I loved what those gifts meant. The rest of that winter, when I was struggling, I would put those socks on, slather myself in the lotion, cup my hands over my face, inhale deeply, and weep. There was healing in the smell of that Jergens. There was healing in wearing those socks. Healing in remembering that I was loved and at least one person thought I was amazing.

A few months ago, while on her way to church to play her keyboard with the worship team, Marian was hit head-on by a drunk driver and went on home to be with Jesus. I came across those socks last week and held them to my face. I cried and laughed. Those used socks will forever be one of the greatest gifts I have received, because they were given with thought and purpose. God had put those socks in Marian's path at just the right time to lift me up when I was in a dark place.

Marian taught me how to look at the world differently. She taught me how to be kind and courageous. She taught me that it was OK to walk a different path and follow my heart, even if I had to walk alone. She was brilliant like a diamond in a bucket of coal. She was truly amazing—even if she didn't have socks that proclaimed it.

Acknowledgments

Every attempt has been made to credit the sources of copyrighted material used in this book. If any such acknowledgment has been inadvertently omitted or miscredited, receipt of such information would be appreciated.

Scripture quotations marked (CSB) are taken from *The Christian Standard Bible*, copyright © 2017 by Holman Bible Publishers. Used by permission.

Scripture quotations marked (ESV) are taken from *The Holy Bible, English Standard Version*. Copyright © 2001 by Crossway Bibles, a division of Good News Publishers. Used by permission. All rights reserved.

Scripture quotations marked (GW) are taken from *GOD'S WORD®*. Copyright © 1995, 2003, 2013, 2014, 2019, 2020 by God's Word to the Nations Mission Society. Used by permission.

Scripture quotations marked (JPS) are taken from *Tanakh: A New Translation of the Holy Scriptures according to the Traditional Hebrew Text*. Copyright © 1985 by the Jewish Publication Society. All rights reserved.

Scripture quotations marked (KJV) are taken from the *King James Version of the Bible*.

Scripture quotations marked (NASB) are taken from the *New American Standard Bible®*, Copyright © 1960, 1971, 1977, 1995, 2020 by The Lockman Foundation. All rights reserved.

Scripture quotations marked (NET) are taken from the *NET Bible®* (New English Translation). Copyright © 1996–2017 by Biblical Studies Press, L.L.C.; http://netbible.com. All rights reserved.

Scripture quotations marked (NIV) are taken from *The Holy Bible, New International Version®*, *NIV®*. Copyright © 1973, 1978, 1984, 2011 by Biblica, Inc. Used by permission. All rights reserved worldwide.

Scripture quotations marked (NKJV) are taken from the *New King James Version®*. Copyright © 1982 by Thomas Nelson. Used by permission. All rights reserved.

Scripture quotations marked (NRSVUE) are taken from the *New Revised Standard Version, Updated Edition*. Copyright © 2021 National Council of Churches of Christ in the United States of America. Used by permission. All rights reserved worldwide.

Scripture quotations marked (RSV) are taken from the *Revised Standard Version of the Bible*. Copyright © 1946, 1952, 1971 by the Division of Christian Education of the National Council of the Churches of Christ in the United States of America. Used by permission.

A Note from the Editors

We hope you enjoyed *Strengthened in Faith*, published by Guideposts. For more than 75 years, Guideposts, a nonprofit organization, has been driven by a vision of a world filled with hope. We aspire to be the voice of a trusted friend, a friend who makes you feel more hopeful and connected.

By making a purchase from Guideposts, you join our community in touching millions of lives, inspiring them to believe that all things are possible through faith, hope, and prayer. Your continued support allows us to provide uplifting resources to those in need. Whether through our communities, websites, apps, or publications, we inspire our audiences, bring them together, and comfort, uplift, entertain, and guide them. Visit us at guideposts.org to learn more.

We would love to hear from you. Write us at Guideposts, P.O. Box 5815, Harlan, Iowa 51593 or call us at (800) 932-2145. Did you love *Strengthened in Faith?* Leave a review for this product on guideposts.org/shop. Your feedback helps others in our community find relevant products.

Find inspiration, find faith, find Guideposts.

Shop our best sellers and favorites at
guideposts.org/shop
Or scan the QR code to go directly to our Shop

Printed in the United States
by Baker & Taylor Publisher Services